Advance praise f
Carter Heyward's
Touching Our Strength:

"This is magnificent. While reading it I sometimes cried out: 'Heresy!' then read the same passage again as the clearest expression of biblical faith. Heyward does not use mystical terminology, yet the whole book testifies to the mystical experience that is at the heart of both religious and sexual life. We have known a long time that God's power is Love and nothing else, but we forgot, often enough, that this power necessarily empowers the lovers of God. Carter Heyward brings this out with feminist anger and strength, with hilarity and clarity."

—Dorothee Sölle, author of *Of War and Love*

"'Moved with pity, Jesus stretched out his hand and touched him . . .' (Mark 1:41). Leprosy as a biblical metaphor has never been more apt. In the age of AIDS Heyward stubbornly, passionately proclaims 'Touch or cease to be human!' White, Western thought, by contrast, has reduced the healing power of shared physicality to pornography. Carter Heyward's work is a sexual theology that evokes the earthy/earthly relational matrix of becoming human, the core of human power to be whole selves-in-relation."

—Susan Thistlethwaite, author of *Lift Every Voice*

Touching Our Strength

OTHER BOOKS BY CARTER HEYWARD

God's Fierce Whimsy (ed.)
Our Passion for Justice
A Priest Forever
The Redemption of God
Revolutionary Forgiveness (ed.)
Speaking of Christ

Touching Our
STRENGTH

*The Erotic as Power
and the
Love of God*

CARTER HEYWARD

1817

Harper & Row, Publishers, San Francisco

New York, Grand Rapids, Philadelphia, St. Louis
London, Singapore, Sydney, Tokyo, Toronto

Grateful acknowledgment is given for use of the following:

From *Sister Outsider: Essays and Speeches,* copyright © 1984 by Audre Lorde. Used by permission of the The Crossing Press, Freedom, CA.

From "Heterosexism: Enforcing Male Supremacy" by Carter Heyward in *The Witness,* April 1986. Reprinted by permission of *The Witness.*

The essay "Heterosexist Theology: Being Above It All" by Carter Heyward first appeared in the *Journal of Feminist Studies in Religion,* Vol. 3, no. 1 (Spring 1987). Reprinted by permission.

From "Conscientious Objector" by Edna St. Vincent Millay. From *Collected Poems,* Harper & Row. Copyright © 1934, 1962 by Edna St. Vincent Millay and Norma Millay Ellis. Reprinted by permission.

FIRST EDITION

Library of Congress Cataloging-in-Publication Data
Heyward, Carter.
   Touching our strength: the erotic as power and the love of God / Carter Heyward.—1st ed.
      p.   cm.
   Includes bibliographical references.
   ISBN 0-06-250396-0
   1. Sex—Religious aspects—Christianity.   2. Homosexuality—Religious aspects—Christianity.   3. Liberation theology.   4. Heyward, Carter.   5. Feminist theology.   I. Title.
BT708.H49   1989   89-45244
261.8'357—dc20   CIP

---

89 90 91 92 93 BANTA 10 9 8 7 6 5 4 3 2 1

I shall die, but that is all
that I shall do for Death.

EDNA ST. VINCENT MILLAY*

---

* From "Conscientious Objector," *Collected Poems* (New York: Harper & Row, 1934, 1962).

CONTENTS

ACKNOWLEDGMENTS

Without some particular people, this book could not have been written: I'm thinking especially of members of my spring 1988 class, "Theology of Sexuality," who learned with me much of what these pages reflect; and especially Ellen Davis, my talented research assistant who taught the course with me and has helped prepare this manuscript for publication. Lisa Hammer, a student intern from the College of the Atlantic, undertook grueling footnote research and managed to maintain a chipper spirit and good humor.

Carol Blanchard, faculty secretary at the Episcopal Divinity School, provided not only her computer skills but also a perceptive interest in this writing project.

The staff at Harper & Row has been supportive in important ways, especially Georgia Hughes, John Loudon, Arla Ertz, and Harriet Crosby.

A number of students, former students, companions, family, and professional colleagues have explored with me various issues addressed here: Brooke Alexander, Chris Blackburn, Webb Brown, Norene Carter, Connie Chandler-Ward, Alison Cheek, Jeannette DeFriest, Ann Heyward Drinkwater, Tom Driver, Marvin Ellison, Bonnie Engelhardt, Robbie Heyward, Samdino Heyward, Sue Hiatt, Lawrie Hurtt, Judy Jordan, Karl Laubenstein, Myung Sook Lee, Barbara Lundblad, Victoria Rue, Susan Savell, Vida Scudder, Pat Shechter, David Siegenthaler, Chris Smith, Teraph, Will Thompson, Demaris Wehr, Sharon Welch, Delores Williams— these friends have made significant contributions to this book.

Mary Hobgood, Diane Moore, Jenny Walters, Linda Brebner, Myke Johnson, Beth Marie Murphy, Jan Surrey, and Ann Wetherilt read all or parts of the manuscript and made helpful suggestions.

Anne Gilson and Rob Gorsline, who for years have been working on many of these same concerns, were present to me and to this project in ways that only they could be.

Jan Surrey, sister sojourner in explorations of mutuality, has helped spark this study's ambience of openness and movement and joy.

Beverly Harrison read the manuscript in its several incarnations and made the sorts of remarkable contributions that could have been made only by a wise and courageous ethicist who is also a beloved friend and companion of many years.

As healing companions, Elly Andujar, Ann Briley, Ann Franklin, Susan DeMattos, Mary Glasspool, Sydney Howell, Peg Huff, Jean Miller, and Diane Moore struggled with me through much of the living of the relational dynamics behind the written page.

None of these folks is responsible for anything I have written here. But each has touched and strengthened this book in ways that have made it what it is. And all are responsible with me for bearing up the lovemaking, which is justicemaking, which is godding in the world we share. For their company, I am enormously grateful.

Carter Heyward
Cambridge, MA
April 1989

Touching Our Strength

INTRODUCTION

I had to prepare for this and
not just by reading Lorde and Weeks and Raymond
or my own stuff
I had to do more than think
about "sexuality"   "theology"   "ethics"

in order to come to this

I had to connect with you
through memories   fantasies   humor
and struggle
sometimes touching
often amazing
always worthy of respect

in order to come

I had to get myself some daffodils
and wait for them to open
and I had to lie down beside by old dog Teraph
and rub some comfort into his worn out legs
and make myself some Mocha Java decaf
with just enough milk to cut the acid

and then I had to sit for the longest time
and remember
Denise   ANC   Black Sash
South Africa
and I had to ask myself how
we are connected to these movements

for survival and joy
and I had to believe that we are

in order to come

I had to write a poem
about hiding some sisters and their cats from the fascists
a love poem it was
and then hold in my heart an image of my month-old niece
my namesake whom I love and have not seen
and spend some painstaking time with friends
and playful time as well
and I had to be alone for a good long while
for my roots to secure

in order to come

I had to make love
and if I had not had a precious woman
to caress my lusty flesh
and bring me open not only to her
but to myself and you
I still would have had to find a way
to enter more fully
the warm   dark   moisture
of One in whose hunger
for survival and passion
for friends   and movement
for justice   and yearning
for touch and pleasure
we are becoming
ourselves.

This book is not about either sex or God as these terms have denoted particular traditional points of reference: to male and female reproductive/pleasure organs and their manipulation, or to an anthropomorphized deity to whom we ascribe absolute power.* It

---

* Please see the Glossary on pages 187–195 for definitions of terms as they are used in this book.

is about sex and God as we are able to re-image both as empowering sparks of ourselves in relation. In the lexicon of these pages, *sexual* refers to our embodied relational response to erotic/sacred power, and *theology* to a critical reflection on the shape of the Sacred in our life together.

I am reflecting on the erotic as our embodied yearning for mutuality. As such, I am interested not merely in a "theology of sexuality"—examining sexuality through theological lenses; but rather in probing the Sacred—exploring divine terrain—through sexual experience. In these pages, with Audre Lorde, I want "to write fire," to be erotic—touching, pressing, making connections, contributing what I can to the forging of that mutuality which characterizes right relation, or justice.[1]

I am attempting to give voice to an embodied—sensual—relational movement among women and men who experience our sexualities as a liberating resource and who, at least in part through this experience, have been strengthened in the struggle for justice for all. Patterns of sexual and gender injustice are linked inextricably to those of racial, economic, and other structures of wrong relation. It follows that the liberation of *anyone* depends on the tenacity of the connections and coalitions we are able to forge together. To do this work, we must be able to envision these connections and embody this tenacity. Just as important, we must be willing to pursue, critically and imaginatively, the truths of our own particular lives-in-relation—the difference, for example, our race-privilege (or lack) makes to how we experience the world; the part played by our class, our gender, our religion, our nation, our sexual desires, and relationships.

To speak of the erotic or of God is to speak of *power in right relation.*[2] This concept will be developed in the pages that follow as foundational to both sexual pleasure and play and to justice-making. Real lovemaking is not simply genital manipulation. Whether in the context of long-term monogamous mutual relationships or of sex play between occasional partners who are wrestling toward right relation, lovemaking is a form of justicemaking.

This is so not only because, in the context of mutuality, sex is an expression of a commitment to right relation; but also because such sexual expression generates more energy (rather than less, apologies to Freud) for passionate involvement in the movements for justice in the world. Lovemaking turns us simultaneously *into* ourselves and *beyond* ourselves. In experiencing the depths of our power in relation as pleasurable and good, we catch a glimpse of the power of right relation in larger, more complicated configurations of our life together. Good sex involves us more fully in the struggle for justice—as, or with, people of color, women, differently abled people, ethnic and religious minorities, elderly people, and other earthcreatures.

My justice concern in these pages is far-reaching and inclusive of people and creatures whose identities and struggles I do not yet (and perhaps never will) know, yet whose well-being matters. I am particularly concerned in this book with *sexual* justice—the most trivialized, feared, and postponed dimension of social justice in western society and, possibly, in the world. I am clear about the western "bias" of my study, as of my life; I am equally certain that sexual injustice, in many forms and on the basis of various customs and mores, is a global sore festering in fear, cruelty, and violence. I am clear also that the christian church has done much to shape and sustain such violence "in the name of God."

As a western christian, I am interested in helping lay to rest the pernicious dualisms between sex and God, sexuality and spirituality, body and spirit, and pleasure and goodness, which historically the church has used to dull the edges of human and divine experience. By literally splitting us in two, the dominant ideology of western culture has rendered us—to the extent we are white male-identified—flattened facsimiles of fully human beings.[3] We have been stripped—spiritually, physically, emotionally, and intellectually—of our capacities to delight in ourselves, one another, the creation, and its holy wellsprings.

In discussing an earlier draft of this manuscript with a group of friends, I was asked by a student who has left the church why I stay in it, given my experience and perception of the pervasive extent to which misogyny (hatred of women) and erotophobia (fear of the erotic) traditionally have characterized christianity.[4]

My immediate, spontaneous response was that being "in" or "out" of the church doesn't make much difference to me anymore— and that my primary interest, spiritually and intellectually, is in helping empower people, especially my sisters, to live their lives fully whether in or out of the church. This was an honest but incomplete response, because I do care about what the church is— or is not—doing on behalf of justice for human and other earth-creatures.

I am working on behalf of institutional transformation, planted in a willful and, I pray, intelligent and faithful refusal to accept the traditional church's "no" to womanpower as sacred and to sexual pleasure as a delightful relational happening that needs no higher justification. I am involved at the margins of the established ec-clesium—but at the roots of the church's doctrine, discipline, and worship—attempting to do my part in recreating the whole in-habited earth.

Increasingly, I understand my vocational "part" to be that of a healer. I write this book to help heal the splits in my own, as well as our corporate, body. I offer these words as a small contribution to the ongoing historical processes of our becoming a well people, inhabitants of a whole earth, in touch with an unbroken Spirit.

Western theologians, like most other "thinkers" in Euroamerican culture, tend to assume that in our work we speak for everyone. It often seems to us a shame, moreover, that so few folks among the largely unaware masses realize how lucky they are to have such wise and generous spokespersons.

The dominant educational system in western society is cemented in assumptions bred in incubators of fear—of difference, unknown-ness, and change. Herein lurks the supposition that there is a single mode of intellectual discourse that corresponds to a uniform set of abstract truths and in which every person must be schooled in order to be "well-educated"—about "sexuality," "religion," or any other issue.[5]

Despite its rhetoric, this mode of intellectual discourse is hardly "objective." To the contrary, it is steeped in the presumption that human intelligence and human goodness (the two are nearly synonymous in "enlightened" morality) can be achieved only through an immersion in the intellectual tenets of classical western culture, an educational process that leads circuitously back to an affirmative valuation of its own tenets.

Among the most fundamental intellectual and moral foundations of this classical culture is that there is an ideal (one, absolute) way of being (divine, human), which human beings approximate (more or less, depending upon gender, race, class, and other "givens") and to which human beings aspire via knowledge and morality.

Behind this astonishing claim is the far-reaching "common sense," cultivated with oblivious ease by those who historically have held the power in place, that the most intelligent philosophers and theologians and the most moral religious and civil leaders are those who speak most universally of what is true and good and who, therefore, are the least distracted by the special interests, needs, and experiences of particular people. In this context, the most knowledgeable are those few who can tell us more and more about less and less until they've told us everything they know about nothing.

In the spirit and emerging tradition of feminist liberation theology, this book is written on the basis of a different set of assumptions about knowledge and learning. I have no desire or intention to follow classical western lines of reasoning in this presentation of what, to the best of my capacity to know, is true and good. I cannot; for to study either sexuality or theology from a classical western perspective would be to begin on the assumption that embodied—sensual, emotional—knowing is in fact ignorance.

From a classical western perspective, feeling is ignorance, an impediment to "objectivity" and thus to knowing what is either true or good. Moreover, as I attempt to show in chapter 4, women-affirming women and openly gaymen and lesbians embody a particular threat to western culture precisely because we are experienced as embodied knowers—full of feelings, sensuality, and subjectivity in our truth-claims.

I begin on the assumption that objectivity is neither the motive nor the result of value-free education. Objectivity is knowledge of what is happening in the actual life experiences of people-in-relation—what is, in fact, true or good for these real people. To speak passionately of such truth or goodness is to speak objectively of human (and, as I will suggest throughout this book, divine) realities.

I begin also on the assumption that objectivity cannot be experienced as a way of learning, or obtained in the form of truth-claims, unless we who learn and teach are clear with ourselves and one another about the biases we bring to our work—including our candor about those whose interests we intend to serve.

I am writing to serve the interests of lesbians and gaymen, especially those who are coming into a sense of pride and delight in an embodied spirituality that, as yet, they may only intuit as a resource of empowerment and liberation.

I am writing also in the service of feminists and womanists—women and men of different colors; lesbian/gay, heterosexual, bisexual, celibate and sexually active—who are committed to making connections between sexuality, spirituality, and the ongoing struggle for justice *for all*.

I am writing finally on behalf of the interests of progressive and radical religious folk—especially, though not exclusively, christians and former christians—who know the debilitating, violent character of the dualistic splits that break our collective body and shatter us, one by one.

My people hold me accountable—responsible for what I say. And there is nothing abstract about "my people": They are my students and my teachers, my friends and lovers, my *compañeras* and colleagues. They have names, faces, commitments, values, problems, questions, feelings, and ideas. With me and with one another, these people are healers, teachers, priests, pastors, counselors, therapists, organizers, politicians, poets, artists, mothers, fathers, daughters, and sons.

Most of those whose names and ways of being I know best live in the United States and Canada. Some live in Europe. Some in Australia, New Zealand, and Asia. Some in southern and central Africa. Many in Nicaragua and elsewhere in Latin America. Most are of anglo heritage. Most are women. Most are present or former christians. And most are middle strata, well educated in classical western culture.

There are many in whose service I hope to be working whom I do not now (and never will) know—a vast number of people, especially women, throughout this and every nation whose bodyselves have been split asunder by structures of sexual and gender injustice. I attempt to hold myself accountable to these people whose lives I personally do not know and cannot well imagine. This I try to do by reminding myself and my reader that my words represent only a fraction, a small part, of a much larger reality—the truths of which are being formed and reformed in every moment of created and creative life in every pocket of this and every world.

Today and forever, each of us has more to learn than to teach. Yet teach we must insofar as we are called forth, by our people, to contribute our particular part to the magnificent and complex, troubled and puzzling, configuration of human experience.

For my part, I am a white anglo southern christian lesbian priest and academic with class roots in middle-strata United States of America. I am teacher and learner, activist and theorist, well educated by life as well as by school in classical and feminist western culture. I am interested in multicultural and global realities, and hope someday to better understand them.

I have been churched, schooled, counseled, and cajoled to conform to basic tenets of western life and discipline. I have been taught to respect teachings by those for whom obedience, compliance with established rules and good order are virtues, while creativity, rebellion, and passion are heresies. I am neither an anarchist nor a rebel who enjoys chaos. But I prefer justice to injustice; and so I do my part from time to time in generating movement, out of which may come some new or renewed, lovely and just possibility for our lives-in-relation.

The limits of a sexual theology written by any one person seem evident to me. We write of ourselves, however much we may try to veil our particularities by not naming the ways in which they shape our research, interpretations, and presentations.

As a liberal scholar, I might wish to ignore the difference my white anglo roots make to my work. I might wish to be color-blind. Truth to tell, I might not know how not to be color-blind in my scholarship. This is the epistemological folly of those who hold the power in place: We do not see well or easily, if at all, the relevance of our particular life experience.

Our blinders enable us to assume the universality of whatever we say about humanity, sexuality, morality, healing, or God. They allow us to continue to live in the lie that our experience is normative for all people—that our lives reflect not merely *a* truth, but *the* Truth.[6]

The fact of the matter is, my racial/ethnic heritage—complete with its legacy of values both positive and negative, as I understand them—plays a major role in shaping this sexual theology. And this is not an apology. It need not be a problem as long as my readers and I are clear about the limits of what we are engaging.

I wish to say to my progressive white friends (who constitute the majority of this readership) that we need not be ashamed of ourselves. We need not know, we cannot know, all the intricate and critical pieces put in place by our race or class or gender. But we need to be aware that our knowledge is constructed in a social context and shaped by many factors. Such awareness, in turn, helps form our knowledge—in this case, of sexual theology, enabling us to know that there are limits to what we know about sex and God.

Knowing our particular social locations and our limits is not only intellectually honest. It is intellectually empowering as a lens through which we may catch a glimpse of what is, paradoxically, universally true—that all people are limited by the particularities of their life experiences. All of us live, reach, touch, act sexually (or do not) on the basis of particular assumptions that serve us well or poorly.

Particularity is the window of all joy, sorrow, and knowledge for all of us. The particularities of my life, race, gender, sexual preference, religion, and so forth are windows into my sexual theology. And while they limit my truth-claims, they also ground and nourish them.

I am looking for a way of speaking and writing of the power that brings us to life and keeps us going, the power that holds up when we can't imagine how we are managing not to collapse. What or who is this source of comfort—our common strength? We look around. We want to know. We want to see, to touch, to taste this power, this source of justice and compassion in our life together. Who, what, is this source of good, this God?

This root of justice, where is it in our lives? How do we experience the Sacred, that which will liberate us from lives that do not connect in mutually empowering ways? That which will awaken our bodyselves, which have been lulled by violence and fear toward deadness, alienated from the erotic possibility of actually living as lovers of one another, ourselves, and the world?

To whom do we turn for help?

We must be careful to whom we turn for this spiritual mentoring. In seeking a strong personal sense of empowerment and "staying power" or faith (for that is what we are looking for, I believe), we all need help. Our neediness is a given, and it is good. But we must choose our helpers carefully. We need folks who, finally, will be our friends. We need sisters and brothers who are clear that the best they can give us is a radical, embodied affirmation of ourselves-in-relation-to-them: the actual experience of our capacity to be in right relation. This is, without a doubt, the most precious gift that can be given by a helper—a teacher, priest, pastor, therapist, friend.

We must be careful not to romanticize our helpers, for this trivializes both them and ourselves. To romanticize is to idealize; it is to trivialize by ignoring complexity. It is to render one-dimensional that which has many dimensions.

Similarly, to romanticize the struggle, whether for justice or sanity, is to negate the bittersweet character of genuine human effort with an artificial sweetener. It is to demand that our helpers, our leaders, be heroes (that which we are not). To romanticize the search for peace of mind or peace on earth, and to trivialize the real-life sisters and brothers who can help us in a particular historical moment, is to construct liberation movements, liberators, and saviors out of fantasies, fears, and projections—rather than out of a commitment to mutually empowering relationships with all people, including our helpers.

Heroes show us who we are *not*. Helpers show us who we *are*. As individual supermen/wonderwomen, heroes diminish our senses of relational, or shared, power. Helpers call us forth into our power in relation and strengthen our senses of ourselves. Heroes have brought us "religion" in many forms—theisms, deisms, atheisms, humanisms, even a variety of feminisms. They have brought us "solutions" (that is what heroes are for) in forms of psychoanalysis, social analysis, cost analysis; and they have brought us a spectrum of political "solutions" to the problems of western democracies ranging from the unfulfilled dreams of "the free white male" to the false promises of "democracy," to the unrealized character of a fully socialized state.

Heroes have brought us causes and crusades, flags and battles, soldiers and bombs. As our liberators and leaders, popes and presidents, bishops and priests, shrinks and teachers, mentors and gurus, heroes have brought us pipedreams and smokescreens and everything but salvation. And this, I am persuaded, is because we tend to search everywhere except among ourselves-in-relation for peace.

Massive doses of spiritual, political, intellectual, and emotional education have supported our habit of expecting salvation either from "inside" ourselves (becoming emotionally and spiritually whole "within" ourselves as the essence of our "identity") or "outside" ourselves (looking to others' identities—priests, rabbis, therapists, mentors, teachers, leaders, representatives of different religious, psychological, economic, or political systems or movements to mirror for us who we are).

Looking inside ourselves, trying to become whole emotionally and spiritually, can be good for us. Looking beyond ourselves for clues, help, and inspiration in figuring out who we are and where we stand can be important. But this search will lead us only further away from ourselves unless it is grounded—radically—in the ongoing relational movement that is giving each of us a shape, a form, an identity that itself is constantly opening, moving, changing in relation . . .

The search for liberation, profoundly personal and political, is an intrinsically relational adventure. We search together. It is our active solidarity with one another that generates our discovery of who we are together and hence of who each of us is by particular name and unique yearnings and special talents.

We are not photographs. The reality of our lives is three-dimensional: Whether we experience ourselves this way or not, we are inherently relational. This is the metaphysics of all that is created. From a philosophical perspective, this is our ontological (essential) state—our way of being, the way of being human, created, and creative. We are born in relation, we live in relation, we die in relation. There is, literally, no such human place as simply "inside myself." Nor is any person, creed, ideology, or movement entirely "outside myself."

We are involved in one another's lives, "all rolled up together" in this world. What is "in" me is not simply "in" me. My feelings, thoughts, commitments, beliefs are not solely mine. They have been/are being shaped in me by forces and factors that are not me at all but that participate in forming me—parents, teachers, friends, enemies, forces known and unknown to me, ancient and modern, near and distant, familiar and alien to my awareness.

You cannot understand me, much less know me, unless you are open to understanding the world that shapes us both.

Similarly, what is "outside" me is not really, entirely, outside me. The world is the crucible of my personal life. I am touched by and touching others. I am formed by and forming people, processes, events, movements, and historical situations over which I may or may not have control and in which I may or may not have any cognitive interest.

I cannot understand, much less love, the world, unless I am open to understanding and loving you.

"We are the boat. We are the sea. I sail in you. You sail in me."[7] This is the truth of our lives, and it is the essence of our goodness.

Margaret Huff is a pastoral psychologist doing pioneering work at the intersection of psychology and feminist liberation theology.[8] Two years ago she introduced me to the important work of five clinicians and theorists at the Stone Center for Developmental Services and Studies at Wellesley College in Massachusetts.[9] These women—psychiatrist Jean Baker Miller, and psychologists Janet Surrey, Judith Jordan, Alexandra Kaplan, and Irene Stivers—are developing a relational approach to mental health that goes beyond the object-relations work of such psychologists as Ronald Fairbairn and Donald Winnicott.[10] Following their empirical and intuitive perceptions, the Stone Center is proposing that, because we become persons literally in and by relation, it is only in "mutually empathic and empowering" relationships that our well-being can be secured and sustained.[11]

Departing from traditional tenets of psychiatry, psychology, and psychotherapy, the Stone Center proposes that a person's mental health is enhanced as she comes more wholly into her relational power rather than as she learns to be a "separate," "autonomous," or "individuated" self. Our growth as persons in relation is facilitated not primarily by differentiating ourselves from one another but by connecting. It is within our connectedness that we are able to recognize and value our differences. As Janet Surrey maintains, "People share a commonality which is beyond similarity."[12]

The Stone Center does not suggest that we remain in bad relationships, but rather that our growth is not served merely by absenting ourselves from abuse of one form or another. Rather, our health derives from being in mutually empathic and empowering relationships. These astute clinicians and theorists are attempting to shift the primary therapeutic emphasis from individuation and separation as locus of personal growth to growth-producing relationships and mutual connectedness.

The proponents of this relational psychology realize the dangers of slipping into the "feminization" of mental health—that is, of implying (with the shapers of patriarchal culture) that the healthiest and best woman lives relationally (for others) rather than independently (for herself). The Stone Center is not suggesting that women should live *for* others or *for* themselves, but rather that all of us should live *with* others. We can help one another live well together.

In their work, relationship does not mean dependency. Rather, according to Jean Baker Miller, a "growth-fostering relationship" is one in which at least five "good things" happen:

Each person feels a greater sense of "zest" (vitality, energy).
Each person feels more able to act and does act.
Each person has a more accurate picture of her/himself and the other person(s).
Each person feels a greater sense of worth.
Each person feels more connected to the other person(s) and a greater motivation for connections with other people beyond those in the specific relationship. [13]

In a word, a growth-fostering relationship is *mutual*.

The Stone Center's work presupposes that all human beings, male as well as female, are born in a relational matrix. Moreover, while women more than men in white western culture have learned to experience the relationality of our lives in the world, neither women nor men have experienced deeply the full, healing implications of what it would mean actually to live as selves-in-relation, different from one another, yet connected as the very root of our humanness.

One of the far-reaching implications of the Stone Center's

groundbreaking efforts is that the absence of mutually empathic and empowering relationships in our lives, as children and adults, rather than active violence against us, may be the root of abuse. Such an implication would challenge radically and creatively the assumption, common among feminist health care professionals, that abuse is fundamentally a problem of violence, of breaking and violating boundaries. Rather, violence is seen by the Stone Center as a problem of *disconnection:* we are cut off from the possibility of mutuality and joy in our most important relationships. This is profoundly true from an ethical perspective.

The ramifications of the Stone Center's work will be staggering if they are worked out more fully in the therapeutic relationship, and if the efforts of these remarkable clinicians and theorists are joined, more and more, by those of women of color, lesbians, working-class and poorer women, and women of sharply diverse life experiences.

The Stone Center's theory has helped me clarify the emotional and pastoral implications of what I am attempting in this book and elsewhere as I wrestle with the experience and concept of God as our power in mutual relation.

Corollaries to the Stone Center's work in contemporary western theology have been simmering for at least fifty years. Much of the contemporary interest in relational theology has roots in the work of jewish existentialist philosopher Martin Buber. Buber saw the moral need for community to be built on the basis of a strong sense of relational bonding between persons, and between persons and other creatures, such as trees. Exploring the essential connectedness of "I" and "Thou," Buber articulated an ontology of relationship in which the self literally is constituted in, by, and through relation.[14]

John Macmurray, the Scottish moral philosopher, elaborated a similar theme, portraying the person and the personal as, by definition, social—relational.[15] To be a person is to be shaped in relation to others in an ongoing, constant, and remarkable process of becoming who one is. To be a person is, moreover, to be constantly shaping others. Like Buber, Macmurray was troubled by the highly individualized character of contemporary western culture, in which the character of the individual "self" (*his* perceptions, ideas, values, agendas, rights and privileges) had become normative in determining goodness and truth.

During the 1970s socialist feminism began to emerge in the United States and Europe as a critique of white western patriarchal culture—in particular, of its idealization of the autonomous white male's right to social and economic power. Patriarchal capitalism, according to such feminists as Zillah Eisenstein, is the pinnacle of white male privilege, in which the white affluent male has a natural right to own and define everything from doctrines of divinity to truths about sexuality to bodies of women.[16]

The works of such theorists as Eisenstein, Sheila Rowbotham, and Beverly Wildung Harrison presuppose the radically relational foundation of human being as implicitly a moral structure with far-reaching economic, social, psychological, and political requirements.

The presuppositions that we live in a relational matrix with one another in the world (regardless of what we may think about it or how we may feel about it), and that we have a common response/ability to live in mutual relation, provide the impetus for feminist/womanist liberation theology among jewish, christian, postchristian, and pagan women and men.[17] Feminist liberation theologians are certainly diverse in our opinions on such issues as images and names of the divine; scriptural authority; the redemptive role and meaning of such figures as Jesus; and the viability of traditional patriarchal institutions as places within which women can remain healthy and creative. Nonetheless, we speak in unison of the primacy of justice, or right relation, as the goal and purpose of our life together on the earth.

Some of us identify this justice with the "righteousness" of the bond between Creator and creatures as well as between and among creatures. For all of us, friendship is a basic way to experience and envision justice. And many of us, feminist and womanist liberation theologians, understand right relation or justice to be a *mutual* relation that generates joy and justice and a desire for more of the relation. All feminist/womanist liberation theologians hold images of right relation as both impetus and goal of the various interrelated movements against oppression and unjust death and for justice and joy.

In this spirit, feminist/womanist liberation theologians experience and celebrate our connectedness to contemporary movements for justice for people of color in the United States and elsewhere; for a more fully socialized and humanizing economic order; for liberation of such countries as Nicaragua, Korea, and South Africa from the tyranny imposed by United States–backed interests; for women of all colors and cultures—our rights to ourbodies/ourselves and to decent, dignified conditions in which to bear and raise children free of filth and violence; for full access to life for differently abled men, women, and children; and for senior people among us (indeed, for ourselves as we age), that all of us may experience ourselves as worthy of respect, friendship, meaningful work, and good play; and for gaymen and lesbians who struggle not merely for tolerance or pity but for affirmation and celebration of our sensual, sexual, loving selves-in-relation.

Ten years ago I was preparing to write my doctoral thesis, and I had decided to try my hand at a constructive "relational theology." My interest had been stimulated by a series of questions that had emerged as I studied the experiences and questions of Elie Wiesel, a "survivor" of the Holocaust.[18] I found myself wrestling with such questions as these: In a world in which evil continues to spread like wildfire over the earth, wreaking terror and abuse, what can we do? How do we know what is good and what is evil in the small, daily places of our lives? How can we liberate ourselves, with one another's help, from evil? What visions do we need to inspire our struggle?

Such questions haunted me then, and they still do. I suspect they always will. Their presence reminds me of a relational spark in myself that I know to be my soul—the core of myself in relation or, from a more traditional perspective, "the seat of God" within me.

In struggling to come to terms with the pervasiveness of evil in our life together—for example with anti-Semitism, racism, heterosexism, economic exploitation, and their violent interconnections—I have become increasingly interested in probing the character of that which is radically good in our commonlife: our power in mutual relation as the basis of our creative and liberating possibilities, literally the only basis of our hope for the world. This interest has produced this sexual theology. *For, at its core, this book is about nurturing and cultivating the goodness in our lives.*

And as we nurture our common goodness, are we better able to deal with evil? Are we wiser, more courageous, more patient with ourselves and others in this world as we learn to take seriously our power for touching the Sacred, our power for creating and sustaining right relation? Does this strengthen our desire, commitment, and ability to make no peace with oppression? Does the experience of mutuality teach us more fully what it means to live serenely— in quiet confidence that, regardless of the toll of violence, betrayal, and evil in our lives, nothing can separate us from the power of good, the power in right relation, which christians and other theists may choose to name "the love of God"?

This book is shaped in the matrix of such questions. I do not know the answers, and I cannot find them by myself. We work together, you and I. We help each other learn to risk, in gentle measure, a day at a time, involving ourselves more fully in healing the splits within, between, and among us. We call each other forth, daring to touch our strength: to participate, with confidence, with awe, and with one another, in the ongoing redemption of God.

Following my earlier academic effort to write personally rather than abstractly, the form of this book also is often more conversational, invitational, and imaginative than expository.[19] Its intellectual roots are in a critical, reflective matrix of spiritual struggle; theological study; social analysis; political commitment; personal passions, fears, dreams, biases; and, of course, in the many relationships that continue to form and reform my capacities to love, learn, and work.

Chapter 1

COMING OUT: COMING INTO OUR *YES*

Madness, not just physical abuse, was the punishment for too much talk if you were female. Yet even as this fear of madness haunted me, hanging over my writing like a monstrous shadow, I could not stop the words, making thought, writing speech. For this terrible madness which I feared, which I was sure was the destiny of daring women born into intense speech . . ., was not as threatening as imposed silence, as suppressed speech.

In retrospect, "talking back" became for me a rite of initiation, testing my courage, strengthening my commitment, preparing me for the days ahead . . .*

For me, coming out to my sexuality goes hand in hand with coming out to my spirituality. I grew up in an orthodox Calvinist home and community where one's options were always limited to one of two things: You were elect or you were reprobate; you were married (sexually active and procreative) or you were single (celibate and lonely); you were good or you were bad; you were right or you were wrong; you were Christian Reformed or you were prone to heresy; you were a success (hardworking) or you were a failure (lazy).

Coming out to my spirituality means that I know I have many options but at this time I can only say that I am spiritual. I cannot identify myself as Christian, neo-Pagan, post-Christian, or Witch. Coming out to my sexuality means that I have many options but at this time I can only say that I am sexual. I cannot identify myself as straight, lesbian, bisexual, or celibate. Coming out is a process.

Maartje, theological student

---

* bell hooks, *Talking Back: Thinking Feminist, Thinking Black* (Boston: South End Press, 1989), 7, 9.

Coming out is a relational process associated with lesbians' and gaymen's public affirmation of ourselves in relation to one another. Coming out of the closet in which our relational lives are kept hidden from public view and, usually, condemnation, we move into a shared power.

Our power is erotic because it is about embodying relational connections. This power is sacred because it is shared. It is transforming because it is creative. And our power is liberating because it moves the struggle for justice. By this power, in this power, and with this power, we find ourselves-in-relation, breaking out of the isolation imposed by silence and invisibility.

As a profoundly relational movement, the coming-out process among gaymen and lesbians can be paradigmatic for all efforts toward right and honest relationships. This chapter is about gay and lesbian experience; but it is also about making mutually empowering connections between and among us all, whoever we are.

Coming out, we well may be drawn into our power in right relation.

I suspect nothing is more heartbreaking to God herself than the denial of our power to recognize, call forth, and celebrate right relation among ourselves.[1] Locked within ourselves, holding secrets and denial, we embody not merely the fear of our relational possibilities; we also embody the rejection of the sacred ground of our being, which is none other than our power to connect.[2]

The fear of mutuality is the fear of our intrinsic interrelatedness, the fact that literally I am nobody without you. Our we-ness creates my I-ness and yours as well. And we fear this creation, this calling forth of ourselves, in this particular social location in the late twentieth century. Our fear of mutuality is embedded in such structures of advanced patriarchal capitalism as marriage, sexual "identity," family, education, business, medicine, religion, psychotherapy.[3] This fear is so deeply structured into our social organization and psyches that we have learned not only to accept it as normal but also to affirm it as a good sign of the healthy self, separate and independent.

In this milieu, white middle-strata women's quest for independence is a slippery slope. For so long we have been the subordinate character in the nonmutual gender structure. We now want out from under. Coming out from under, we must be careful not to set ourselves against the realization that we need one another.

We do not need more domination and submission. We do not need to be shaped, named, and governed by others or patronized by those who believe they know what's best for us. But we need one another, and never more so than now. Surely the strongest foundation of feminism is in our discovery that we are not alone. In struggling with one another for survival, sanity, serenity, and senses of self, we find ourselves: women, sisters, friends.

Coming out of the chilly delusion that personhood is autonomous, breaking free of the notion that self-possession should be our personal and professional goal, we come into our power to call forth the *YES* that connects us—our erotic energy: our sensual and sexual yearnings, our openness to sacred movement between and among ourselves.[4] Coming out, we invite each other through veils of fear set between us for generations. Learning how to love one another, we find our bodyselves opening to a realm of life, confidence, and power we had not dared, alone, to believe in. And this opening is prayer.

Theology, the study of God, can be defined in various ways. I define it as critical, creative reflection on the patterns, shape, and movement of the Sacred in our life together, and I go further: The pattern of the Sacred in our life together is justice. The shape of God is justice. The movement of the Holy in our common life is toward justice. The justice of God is both with us now and coming.

But what is justice? I invite you to think beyond the images of jurisprudence and legalism often associated with justice in patriarchal, androcentric society into a realm of radical relationality. In this realm, justice is right relation, and right relation is mutual relation. In a mutual relationship both (or all) people are empowered to experience one another as intrinsically valuable, irreplaceable earthcreatures, sources of joy and love and respect in relation to one another. To experience ourselves genuinely as friends: This is justice. It is the shape of God in our life together and in our lives as particular selves-in-relation.

Praxis is the constant interplay of theory and action in every moment of our lives. To be asked about our theological praxis is to be asked where we're grounded theologically—what we do, not just what we think, about God. But it is also to be asked what we think. Good critical, creative thinking is grounded honestly in the real-life stuff of changing diapers, shoveling snow, having sex, being cold on the streets. . . . Good theological thinking about such things is revolutionary work. The closer we get to home, the places of our lives, the more revolutionary may be our praxis.

I sometimes use the term *relational matrix* for our place of origin, our common home, all of us earthcreatures. It's a way of imaging what Martin Buber means when he writes "in the beginning is the relation"—not "God" as conceptualized alone, by himself, in need of nothing, invulnerable, the one who moves but is never moved.[5] Such a god is not "in the beginning" and certainly is not a source or resource of love. Love is a mutual dynamic in which lover and beloved are empowered and empowering, literally re-creating one another.

From a trinitarian perspective (though a far cry from what fathers of the church have in mind), we may try to envision, on the basis of our experience, God in three images: God is our relational matrix (or womb). God is born in our relational matrix. God is becoming our relational matrix.[6]

God is our relational power—our power in mutual relation. It is from this God that you and I draw our power to be in life in the first place, and to sustain our lives in relation. In sustaining and becoming ourselves in relation, we are giving birth to more of this same sacred power who needs us, her friends, to bring her to life and help nourish her life on the earth.[7] She is being born among us, and yet she is seldom fully present, fully herself. To that extent, she is not yet but becoming. Where there is brokenness, fear, despair, or violence, the power may not be—yet. But with our help, she is becoming.

The image of God in relation to evil can be envisioned as real only insofar as we experience the radicality of our relational, collective life together. For none of us on this earth—past/present/future, and not Jesus himself—has the power to overcome despair, brokenness, and violation. Only together, hands joined and bodies leaning into one another, is there hope for this world and any of us in it.

God is our relational power. God is born in this relational power. God is becoming our power insofar as we are giving birth to this sacred Spirit in the quality of our lives in relation, the authenticity of our mutuality, the strength of our relational matrix.

It is a paradox: God is becoming our relational matrix insofar as we are the womb in which God is being born. This may be easier to comprehend if we substitute the word "love" for "God." Love is becoming our relational matrix if we are the womb in which love is being born. Love is becoming our home if we are lovers. God is becoming our power in relation to the extent that we are coming into our power as lovers of one another.

We can come into our power as lovers by coming out. There is great power in naming ourselves. For you to come out will contribute to the well-being of us all insofar as you are participating in shaping the Sacred among us. But how do we join in sustaining this holy power in the world? In what ways can we care genuinely for ourselves and one another?

How can this happen in a society in which lesbians and gaymen who are honest about our sexuality are perceived correctly to embody a challenge to the prevailing order of power-relations in the dominant culture?

The way is a passionate one of helping one another learn to bear and sustain creatively—at times even joyfully and gratefully—the real and daily tensions in our lives between, for example, our desire for our own well-being and our commitment to the well-being of others. This creative bearing up of tension among us is our passion.

I feel passionately my erotic movement in relation to others. I know that, in relation, I am a dynamic, sensual organism. I am bounded by my skin—porous, open, and fluid, with holes larger and smaller through which I take in and put out what I must to live, and through which, with my permission, others may also pass from time to time, sensually or sexually, with me.

My eroticism is my participation in the universe. As Pierre Teilhard de Chardin writes, "The Body is the very universality of things. . . . My matter is not a part of the universe that I possess totally. It is the totality of the universe that I possess partially."[8]

But we must be careful. A hermeneutic (interpretive principle) of suspicion demands that we be suspicious even of our own assumptions and of ways in which what we hold to be true, moral, or good can be distorted. For example, to speak of our bodyselves as not being our own possession or of belonging to the whole universe can be dangerous and damaging. Women have never had a socially established, religiously affirmed, physically safe, or emotionally secure sense of our own body integrity. We have not known or loved our bodyselves *as our own*, for we have no control over who or what passes into or out of us. One of the basic historical tenets of patriarchal social relations, sustained by demands of late-capitalist economic conditions, is that women's bodies must be controlled in order for the society to function properly—that is, to maximize profit for the wealthy.

No theological claim can be taken abstractly as true. Even the most apparently benign statement, such as "God is love," can be used as an impetus or justification for such reprehensible moral ends as lynchings, gassings, rape, wife-battering, or child abuse. No theological statement stands on its own. Our theologies are accountable to justice. We meet truth, we encounter the Sacred, we know God, only in the actual living of life a day at a time.

Our theological language bears witness to the truths of our experience and vice versa. We must hold ourselves and one another accountable for our faith-claims.

Occasionally a lesbian or gayman will say that she or he must come out to have integrity. This is fine, provided that by "integrity" the person does not mean to portray herself or himself as a whole, integrated self apart from others. Integrity is not a self-possession. We become fully ourselves—our wholeselves—insofar as we are trying to live in right, mutual relation to others. Integrity is a relational blessing, given as we become centered, at home, in the particularity of who we are—as lesbian, white, christian, alcoholic.

This means that we can never live simply "for ourselves." Nor can we live simply "for others." Women in particular must not allow our integrities to be formed by the spurious lesson we have been taught that we should be more for others than for ourselves. To live with integrity, we live *with* others: We are "for" ourselves and "for" others. In fact, the more we are genuinely for others, the more we are authentically for ourselves; and the more we are for ourselves, the more we are for others.

In the daily realm of love and friendship, we seldom face a zero-sum choice. The more I love you, the better able I am to love myself, and vice versa. In living this paradox, we help each other sustain creative tension between what we often think of as our own needs in relation to the needs of others.

Our respective needs or desires may appear to be competitive, even mutually exclusive: My desire to be close may seem antithetical to your wish for space and distance. Yet, between us, in honoring not only ourselves and each other but also the relational process, we often can find a way to honor each of our yearnings to an extent greater in its effect than either of us might have imagined.

Janet Surrey calls this process "taking care of the relationship."[9]

From a theological perspective, taking care of the relationship presupposes a spiritual goodness inherent in the movement toward right
relation. This goodness, or God, is our power in right relation.

We cannot come out in such a way as to do justice to anyone
if we cannot discern connections between our own sense of hap-
piness and well-being and that of others—parents, children, lovers,
spouses, friends, colleagues. We cannot come out perfectly. We
cannot make everyone happy. We cannot make everyone feel good.
We cannot make everyone agree with us that our sexuality is good,
or that our relationships are good, or that our divorce is good.

We can be aware that everything we say, do, choose, or refuse
to choose affects us and others. Our words do, and our silence
does. We can use words and silences in a spirit of profound respect
for ourselves and others, including those who remain captive to
their own fears.

In this tension between self and others, we can learn *with* others
gradually how to embody both an active indignation with injustice
and a sense of patience with individuals who may be more
frightened than we are. We learn only with one another's help to
experience anger and compassion, not as opposites or contradictions
but as essential dimensions of love.[10]

The choice to remain silent is as much a choice as the choice
to come out. Just as it is possible to speak publicly about one's
sexuality in a way that is damaging to oneself or others, it is possible
to remain silent about one's sexuality in ways or for reasons that
are wrong. The morality of either choice is contingent upon the
tension between self and others being sustained with wisdom and
courage.

For me to come out as a lesbian, whether or not I would wish
it, is to make my sexuality a major issue in my life. I believe that
the celebration of the erotic and of our desire to express it sexually
ought to be a major issue in our life together because it is the
primary wellspring of our capacity to be creative together—to love
one another, write poetry, struggle for justice and friendship.

When I came out as a lesbian, many people asked, "Why put limits on how you're going to be perceived? Why box yourself in? Don't you know that folks are going to think this is all you are— a lesbian, and that all lesbians do is fool around under the sheets together? What about your interests in Latin America? in the work of Elie Wiesel? in christology? Why do you want people to think that sexuality is all you can talk about?"

I knew that I was still interested in Elie Wiesel and in El Salvador and in struggling against racism and in jogging and walking the dog. . . . Perhaps because I was already reasonably well established as a dissonant voice within my professional circles, as priest and theologian, I have not experienced myself as perceived by most people solely on the basis of my lesbian identity.

Still I would be lying or foolish to suggest that a lesbian who comes out can continue business as usual. She cannot. We cannot. But then why would we want to? Do we not come out precisely in order to disrupt the status quo? To come out as a lesbian or gayman is to make our sexuality a (possibly the) central factor in our public world. To come out without realizing this is irresponsible.

I knew in 1979 (though not as well as ten years later) that what we do sexually is related to what we are doing, for example, in Latin America. Both are about *power*—how it is used or abused among us. As I began to see more clearly how this is so, I began to know myself as empowered and empowering in particular relational configurations, and as disempowered and disempowering in others.

In relation to her jewishness, Adrienne Rich writes, "I had never been taught about resistance, only about passing."[11] To some extent, when I came out in 1979, I knew that my coming out was an act of resistance to unjust power relations, unjust gender relations in particular. I did not realize at the time, however, how fundamentally these unjust power relations are interstructured into our lives on the basis of gender, sexual preference, race, religion, age, ablebodyism, culture, ethnicity, nationality, and so on.

It has been far easier for me to be "out" as a lesbian since I began to understand, in my own life experience as well as through the lives of others, that the ways in which sexual power is used and abused among us are connected to the ways in which religious, economic, racial, and other forms of power-over, or power as control, are exercised.

I see now what I saw less clearly a decade ago: The same motive that urged me out of the closet also draws my attention to what's happening in Nicaragua, invites me to do feminist liberation christology, and sparks my interest in Elie Wiesel's work. The motive is a decision to cast my lot with those who resist unjust power relations—in our most intimate relationships, in our work, in the more explicitly public and political arenas of our life together.

In 1979, part of me still wanted to "pass." Today I am clear that I don't pass in relation to the norms of dominant political, theological, or psychological culture. Slowly, I am learning to live not in disappointment but, rather, gratefully at the margins. Coming out moves me further, a day at a time, into the realization that I don't want to pass.

This has been the most liberating, creative, and painful lesson of my life. I have learned it in an educational matrix with friends and lovers, students and teachers, therapists and *compañeras*, all sorts of human and other earthcreatures. With these sisters and brothers, I have been learning to trust the authority of those voices, my own and others, which call us more fully into mutually empowering relation.

I have experienced a difficult tension between revelation and concealment of myself. I was raised to "tell the truth." This little moralism has served me well in many ways, such as in my decision to come out as a lesbian, a decision I have not regretted. Today, however, I see how little I knew when I came out about taking care of myself emotionally, spiritually, and physically. It is possible, I am learning, both to take care of ourselves and to take public stands. Possible and very hard.

There is profound theological wisdom in the tension between

revelation and concealment: The Sacred reveals herself to us when we are ready to see her—ready, that is, to see more clearly ourselves in right relation. God is, however, in our midst continually, whether or not we are ready to notice her. Prophets always appear when God is ready and we are not. In such moments, the sacred Spirit may not be evident to us. She even may seem to be a bother, a nuisance, a problem. The wisdom of God is not always evident to us, not always revealed, because we are not always ready to see what is happening.

Because we cannot bear so much reality, God's presence is often concealed from us: We do not realize what is good until we are ready to help generate the conditions for it. Yet the knowledge of God can be called forth. It is available to us whenever we are ready. What we do not see now also is important to our knowing and caring for ourselves, one another, and our relationships. Revelation—of divinity and of the fullness of humanity—is a matter of timing, of seasoning our capacities to risk seeing and showing forth our goodness when we are ready to live into what we see.

And in the hidden places of our lives, preparations can be made even now toward enabling us to respond to those kairotic moments in which the time will be right for us to open ourselves more fully to one another and to the larger world. Like bread, we are being prepared to rise.

Whenever we speak the truths of our lives in situations in which our truths are unwelcome, we are like intense light, difficult for others to bear. The primary danger to us is that the intensity of our own light may bounce back upon us and blind us. In coming out, we do not know any more than others about how to live the implications of our lives as openly lesbian women or gaymen.

How do we live well, responsibly, and joyfully as lesbians or gaymen in heterosexist, homophobic society? How do we live the implications of our own lives? The light we shed critically on our society shines upon us no less, and we may find ourselves exposed and vulnerable. Like everyone in this society, we are frightened of what it means to be gay or lesbian. As lesbians or gaymen, we are frightened of being feared, rejected, hated, or killed. We are also confused about the full implications of living publicly as happy faggots or dykes in the world/church/synagogue. In this situation, some measured concealment and carefully refracted light is often wise.

The tension between revelation and concealment can be illuminated by recasting it as a pull between taking a stand here and now and sustaining the longer-term, ongoing process of coming out. It is a matter of keeping faith in our interrelatedness and in the power of our relation, and thereby of living in a confidence that, if not now, then later; and if not me, then others, representing me.

This is radically relational faith. It enables us simultaneously to take a stand here and now and to wait for the Spirit to move us along into a future we cannot control, a future that will be shaped by all of us, not just by one or two.

The ongoingness of the coming out process, the sustaining of experienced tensions between self and others, sexuality and other dimensions of ourselves, revelation and concealment, now and later, takes an enormous toll on us all—especially when our faith in the power of our relation to one another is flagging.

And you whose spirits are sad or unsure, try to remember the very best parts of your life, the loveliest feelings in your bodyself, occasions of bold delight and quiet confidence, moments of unambivalent commitment and unrestrained joy. Try to remember when you have believed passionately in something or someone, human or divine. Try to imagine that someone now believes in you because she trusts your loveliest feelings . . . commitments . . . confidence . . . joy. *She is your friend, whether or not you would have her, for she calls forth the best in you.* She comes in the knowledge that together you, she, and others embody a moving image of sacred power, a fresh wellspring of relational integrity. *She goes with us as we are called forth to go, with one another,* evoked by historical memory and by voices audible only to ears that can hear the power of God in history. Her name is love.

We also experience tension between our clarity and our confusion about coming out, about our sexualities, about ourselves in general. This pull is essential in our coming out. Most lesbians and gaymen who are coming out value clarity. But we ought not to underestimate the positive, constraining, and dynamic role of confusion in our lives.

By confusion, I mean that which is unclear, cloudy, unable to be seen well at this time. It is a form of concealment. Among lesbians and gaymen, confusion is bred into our experience of dominant power relations in the world/church. These heterosexist relations, after all, have shaped us in their image. Coming out of them, we are bound to be mystified, for we literally are coming out of ourselves as we have been shaped by heterosexist ideology and have come to know and recognize ourselves as either mad or bad in relation to heterosexist assumptions.

Every healthy lesbian and gayman, every feminist woman and person of color in the United States, has at one time or another been profoundly confused about his or her sense of worth in our society. Regardless of how strong and well grounded we are, our confusion about ourselves will sometimes outweigh our clarity. We need to honor our confusion and let it be in order to move gradually through it. This involves living patiently in the dialectic between confusion and clarity as we attempt to pace ourselves in coming out.

We also experience tension between the desire to express sexually our yearning for mutuality and our efforts to stay in control of our bodyselves. Coming out involves being stretched between these urges—to come into a wild, erotic ecstasy, a full celebration of our bodyselves and those of others; and, at the same time, to hold on to ourselves, keep the lid on, lest we simply disintegrate in the midst of a culture hostile already to who we are.

We need to be gentle with one another and ourselves. We must be careful not to move too far ahead of ourselves; and, when we do, we need to be patient with one another and ourselves as we try again to find our relational rhythms. Coming out in heterosexist patriarchy is a lifetime project. We need lots of time and space to feel, and become aware of, the radical significance of living as openly gay and lesbian people.

The relational self is a matrix in which the Sacred is being born insofar as we are sustaining these tensions. In this way, our body-selves become the ground upon which God moves through, with, and among us.

The divine presence is incarnate—embodied—in our relational selves. Our power in relation is being shaped in the matrix of each relational self who is true to herself as relational. The justice of God, alive in us insofar as we are true to ourselves, is reflected by the mutuality in our relationships with one another, which in turn enable us to sustain creatively the tensions in which the Sacred is at home among us.

To know this deeply within ourselves is serenity.

Our sexualities are our embodied yearning to express a relational mutuality in which the tensions are sustained, not broken.

Sexual orgasm can be literally a high point, a climax in our capacity to know, ecstatically for a moment, the coming together of self and other; sexuality and other dimensions of our lives; a desire for control and an equally strong desire to let go; a sense of self and other as both revealed and concealed; the simultaneity of clarity and confusion about who we are; and tension between the immediacy of vitality and pleasure and a pervasive awareness, even in moments of erotic ecstasy, that the basis of our connection is the ongoing movement—that is, the friendship—that brings us into this excitement and releases us into the rest of our lives, including the rest of this particular relationship.

There is remarkable erotic power in these tensions. To stretch and pull with one another is to come more and more into our erotic possibilities, into a fullness of ourselves in mutual relation, in which the Sacred is being born among us.

The implications of sexual godding for our love and work are foundational because, in this society, we have two things in common: our immersion in nonmutual power relations and our desire for a better way.

Our lives have deep, decadent roots in unjust power relations. These have obscured in countless ways our capacities even to believe in the possibility of mutual relation (except, if we are lucky, in a few very special relationships). Even feminist professionals—ministers, therapists, teachers, for example—need throughout our lives to help one another move out of the structures of nonmutual power relations that have secured our professions, shaped our psyches, and still do. Despite our commitments to justice, we do not know how to love one another very well.

As a description of how we experience relational power, mutuality does not necessarily imply equality, nor does equality assure mutuality. Equality denotes a sameness of position or status, while mutuality describes a dynamic relational movement into a vision of ourselves together.

The vision of mutuality often includes equality between, for example, people of different races or men and women. But the vision is of more than mere equality. It is a vision of justice in which, by the power of God, we call one another forth into our most liberating, creative possibilities. Mutuality, unlike equality, signals relational growth and change and constitutes an invitation into shaping the future together.

There are many relationships in which unequal power is the consequence of systemic alienation—for example, between white and black people and between men and women. In such relationships, mutuality can be difficult to sustain; but without it, the relationships are abusive.

The bond between a parent and child is, optimally, one of temporary inequality, in which the mutuality in the relationship generates conditions for growth in both equality and mutuality. Unless it is a mutual relationship, in which both are growing and changing in relation to each other, the parent-child bond is abusive.

There are also relationships, such as that between a therapist/ counselor and client/counselee, in which unequal power is, for a period of time, structured emotionally, as well as financially, into the relationship. This structure of temporary inequality has a primary purpose: to enable the counselee to experience herself, increasingly, as empowered in relation to others, including her counselor.[12] In order for this to happen, the counselor also must be changed in the relationship; she too must be able to be touched and moved by the relational process.

Thus the aim of a "helping" relationship is for those in it to generate the emotional as well as material conditions for, sometimes, more equality (for example, the client might become the therapist's teacher; they might become colleagues or friends) and *always* for more mutuality. That is to say, both people should be growing and changing in the relationship, mutually empowered to become more fully themselves with one another.

In any unequal power relationship, if the structure of inequality is assumed to be static (as in all racist or sexist relations, as well as in traditional modes of church leadership and psychotherapy), the relationship cannot enable authentic empowerment. If, moreover, the effects of inequality are presumed, and even encouraged, to linger *in perpetutity* (as in all patriarchal, nonmutual relations, including those steeped in ecclesiastical and therapeutic traditions), the relationship will be emotionally and spiritually distorted for both, regardless of how well meaning they may be.

Any unequal power relationship is intrinsically abusive if it does not contain seeds both of transformation into a fully mutual relationship and of mutual openness to equality. Individual goodwill and professional competence cannot solve systemic and historical problems of intrinsically abusive power relations. Our lives have damaged and damaging roots in relational assumptions that we have learned by living, and which all of us perpetuate to some extent. But we have in common also a yearning for mutually empowering relations. We have our sexualities, as we actually experience ourselves and as we long to experience ourselves. Audre Lorde writes, "We have been taught to fear the YES within ourselves, our deepest cravings."[13]

Coming out is a way of coming into our YES.

Chapter 2

NOTES ON HISTORICAL GROUNDING: BEYOND SEXUAL ESSENTIALISM

Our history is inseparably part of our nature, our social structures are inseparably part of our biology.

—JOAN L. GRISCOM*

From my "Holiness" Christian background, complete with sexual taboos, I discovered and hid in puberty the pleasure of masturbation, a delicious bathtime/bedtime thrill. Fantasies and pictures of Marilyn Monroe were hidden too, and I was constantly convicting myself of the sinfulness of my nightly obsession.

I began dating after I left my parsonage home for college. I thrilled at the first touch of a woman's thigh. I fell in love repeatedly and ached for intimacy. But at my religious college, my few serial loves considered sexual exploring ("feeling them up") to be prurient—and spiritual exploring was unheard of. I was rejected by a woman (to whom I had proposed marriage) because of my "weird" ideas—like seeing nothing wrong with sex as long as she didn't get pregnant.

After a stint in the factory, as a graduate student in philosophy at a midwestern university, I blossomed. I saw movies, drank beer, smoked pot, and fell in love twice again. I discovered sexual intimacy with each of these women, and they marveled at the wonder with which I

---

* Joan L. Griscom, "On Healing the Nature/History Split," in *Women's Consciousness/Women's Conscience*, edited by Barbara H. Andolsen, Christine E. Gudorf, Mary D. Pellaeur (San Francisco: Harper & Row, 1985), 97.

touched their bodies. Yet, despite my devotion, each left me.

For the next seven years, I explored a number of liaisons, sharing sexual intimacy in most but finding no lasting spiritual connection. Beginning to practice Buddhist prayer, I enlarged my agenda from only desires for sexual intimacy to attention to the others' depths of concern. . . .

Sexual relationships became fewer. In 1982, after six years of Buddhist fellowship, I was expelled by my fellow Buddhists for theological questioning, and I became so-·cially isolated.

Grant,
theological student

Our sexual relations, indeed our sexual feelings, have been shaped by historical forces—the same contingencies, tensions, politics, movements, and social concerns that have shaped our cultures, value systems, and daily lives.

In *The Handmaid's Tale,* Canadian Margaret Atwood portrays with chilling, imaginative insight the centrality of sexual control in the new christian fundamentalist nation of Gilead, formerly the United States: White women are forced to breed and are forbidden to have sex except with the Commanders, the white men who own them. Gaymen and lesbians are summarily executed. Black people are ghettoized in Detroit. These are the very forces about which social anthropologist Gayle Rubin speaks: "The right has been spectacularly successful in tapping [the] pools of erotophobia in its accession to state power."[1]

Good social history is written not just from the perspective of "the winners." It teaches us about the connections between the control of women's bodies for procreation; the suppression of homosexuality; the economic system and conditions of a particular place and time; the virulence of such social forces as racism and anti-Semitism; and the exercise of social control by institutional custodians of such normative "virtues" as spiritual growth, mental health, and physical well-being.

It would be small solace for us to imagine that we are nearing the end of a period of blatant political reaction against sexual and gender justice in the United States. Even if this were superficially the case, the radicality of the injustice in our power relations goes deeper than any one political party or heyday of the religious right. The problems in our sexual and gender relations are historical, they are critical, and they connect us all.

A historical reading of sexuality is a reading about power in relation, specifically about how people historically have or have not embodied our capacities for mutually empowering relationships.[2] The study of sexuality is also an exploration of how the exercise of power-over (power-as-control by kings, customs, corporations, gods, and so forth) has shaped our capacities and incapacities to act mutually.[3]

We use and abuse power in relationships. We also are used and abused in relationships. Our capacity to act as cocreative subjects in the dynamics of mutually empowering relations is affected, and determined in some cases, by how we have been objectified and acted upon in our significant relationships. An example of the connection between how we are treated and how we treat others and ourselves is the large extent to which abusive adults have been battered and abused as children.

The late French structuralist Michel Foucault (and, with him, radical British social historian Jeffrey Weeks and feminist liberation theologians in the United States such as Sharon Welch and Beverly Harrison) insisted that no experience of power, sexual or other, is intrinsic to a person or to a relationship, but rather that our experiences of power-in-relation are socially constructed. Sexuality is socially constructed. (The construction of alienated sexuality is discussed more fully in chapter 3.)

For example, few people in Euroamerican culture are strangers to feelings of sadomasochism in our social relations, including our sexual relationships, regardless of how we may act. Ours is a society fastened in dynamics of control and subjugation. None can escape the psychosexual or spiritual fallout of such a system.[4]

In an appreciative but unapologetic critique of such sexologists as Havelock Ellis, Jeffrey Weeks charges, "Possibly the most potent of their legacies is what is now generally known as 'sexual essentialism.' " Weeks is referring to "ways of thinking which reduce a phenomenon to a presupposed essence—the 'specific being,' 'what a thing is,' 'nature, character, substance, absolute being'—which seeks to explain *complex* forms by means of an identifying inner force or truth."[5]

A historical reading of sexuality will move us beyond sexual essentialism as explanation of anything, including either homosexuality or heterosexuality. If we accept a relational, historical matrix as our origin, the womb of who we are becoming, we will not fall into believing that either our identities or our relational possibilities are fixed and unchanging. This is because relationality—the basis of historical agency—presupposes relativity: All of us, and all of everything, is relative to everything else—changing, becoming, living, and dying in relation.

There can be nothing static in a personal identity or relationship formed in such a matrix. There is no such thing as a homosexual or a heterosexual if by this we mean to denote a fixed essence, an essential identity.[6] There are rather homosexual and heterosexual people—people who *act* homosexually or heterosexually.

Relationality relativizes our essence. We are only who we are becoming in relation to one another. Self-knowledge is steeped in awareness of movement and change.

Because history involves change and movement, understanding our sexualities involves knowing in what ways our sexualities are changing and in being open to changing understandings of our sexualities as we continue to learn about our bodyselves. Not only are we not living in the nineteenth century, we are not living in the 1950s or 1960s in terms of how we may experience nutrition, sexual activity, pregnancy, disease, and other bodyself phenomena.

Understanding our sexualities historically involves understanding ourselves as people whose sexualities are in flux.

A historical rather than an essentialist perspective on sexuality involves framing our sexual ethics around issues of what we *do* rather than of what we *are*: What we do as hetero/homosexual persons—how we act in relation to lovers and friends—is the stuff of sexual ethics, rather than whether it is right or wrong to *be* heterosexual or homosexual.

A historical reading of sexuality may make living as lesbians and gaymen more difficult, because we cannot plead for acceptance on the basis of being something we can't help and therefore of needing special sets of rights and understanding because we are homosexuals who didn't choose to be who we are. When we are clear with ourselves and others that our sexual identities are not "essential" but rather are being shaped by many factors, including our own "permission," the difficulties we may incur politically will be offset by our own shared sense of the relational power born among us as we call each other forth and help shape each other's identities.

We no longer have to wage our campaigns for "rights" on the basis of being homosexuals who can't help it because it's just the way we are. Rather, whether we are heterosexual or homosexual, we expect our society to offer basic conditions of human worth and self-respect to *all* people, regardless of sexual preference.

A historical reading of our sexualities that is rooted in our assumption of responsibility for what we do demands responsible engagement from others. It is easy enough for many christian liberals to "love" gaymen, lesbians, divorced women and men, single parents, people with AIDS. It is harder, but more honest and of deeper social value, for us to engage one another's lives in a spirit of mutual respect and discovery. And what better definition of love?

A historical perspective on sexuality is important also because such a view enables us to envision and perhaps experience our own possibilities as sexual persons beyond the constraints of any particular failure in historical imagination—whether the failure be religious, psychological, economic, or cultural.

Dorothee Sölle writes of *phantasie*, a creative mix of intuition and imagination that enables us to participate in shaping the future even as we are grounded in the present.[7] Our *phantasie* helps us experience and understand sexuality as an open, changing, relational dynamic. Our sexual future is not set or predetermined. We are involved in shaping our own dreams.

A historical reading of sexuality moves us beyond sexual essentialism toward understanding ourselves radically as persons-in-relation. We move through *phantasie* toward questions that we would miss altogether unless we were thinking historically, such as Jeffrey Weeks's question about when heterosexual behavior became an ideology—when it began to develop into "compulsive heterosexuality" or "heterosexism." No one knows the answer to this question; but it is interesting and it could become a locus of historical inquiry further into connections between sex, women, and political control.[8]

The christian church plays the central formative role in limiting and thwarting our sexual *phantasie*, or sexual imagination. Most historians, sexologists, and others who are interested in how sexual practices and attitudes have developed historically seem to agree that in the realm of sexual attitudes, western history and christian history are so closely linked as to be in effect indistinguishable.[9] That is to say, the christian church has been the chief architect of an attitude toward sexuality during the last 1,700 years of European and Euroamerican history—an obsessive, proscriptive attitude, in contrast to how large numbers of people, christians and others, have actually lived our lives as sexual persons.

The church's antisexual preoccupation dates from early in the church's history. The Council of Elvira (Spain), at which for the first time an explicitly antisexual code was made law for western christians, was held in 309 C.E. This was on the eve of the Constantinian settlement, in which the church formally made its peace with the state and in so doing lost a major element of its identity: its role as a body of resistance to oppressive power relations.

Historical theologian Samuel Laeuchli writes of the Council of Elvira:

In the turmoil of a decaying empire the Christian Church attempted to find its communal identity; in the crisis that had come about at the twilight of antiquity, the Christian elite [bishops and presbyters] sought to carve out a clerical image. Both of these struggles rose to the surface whenever the synod of Elvira dealt with matters of sexuality. By establishing sexual codes the synod meant to define the particular character of Christian life; by setting sexual taboos, the synod meant to create the image of an ascetic clerical leadership. . . . [these texts] were of far reaching import for the history of Christianity. Few ancient texts provide such evidences and opportunity to examine the purpose behind the Christian elite's antisexual drive as do these canons.[10]

Laeuchli goes on to suggest five reasons why the church's elite became preoccupied with sexual control of the clergy and, to a lesser extent, the laity. First, the need to carve out a new identity for christians as the old identity (of contending against the state) faded into oblivion. Second, the determination on the part of the clergy to establish themselves as powerful in a new sociopolitical context in which christian laity would be looking to Roman leadership as locus of power. Third, the overwhelming emotional and physical demands of becoming part of the Roman world in its expansive, urbane environment. Fourth, the disquieting urbanization of christians who, as increasing numbers became city dwellers, lost their tribal and rural ties. And finally, the breaking apart of religious mythology, both pagan and christian, as the claims of each relativized the other. Laeuchli writes,

It is no coincidence that the second-century movement which so desperately tried to recover the mythological canopy, namely Gnosticism, picked Genesis 3, the idea of a fall, as the starting point for its remythologication in which sexual copulation belongs to heaven, as an abstract cosmic event beyond human reach. Nor is it a coincidence that the philosophical parallel to Gnosticism, middle Platonism . . . , declared body and matter as evil. When man began to lose his secure place in the mythic-cosmic structure which he had hewn for himself, he was thrown into crisis. Perhaps he lost his place because he became urban, and thus conscious of man's universal predicament. No matter what caused this crisis, the bishops and presbyters of Elvira, as the leaders of an exclusive religion, offered an alternative which reckoned with the sexual dilemma of their age.[11]

Ideas, or philosophical possibilities, are seeded in social realities—political, economic, and so on. In periods of social unrest, theologians historically have idealized the human condition by spiritualizing it. At Elvira, this spiritualization took the shape of calling men (it was addressed to males by males) to rise spiritually above their sexual bodies.

Laeuchli's primary thesis is that the church's ordained leadership tightened the sexual reins of the church during a period of confusion and chaos. It was the only control they had. Moreover,

the decisions of Elvira show. . . a crisis in male identity. In the image of manhood which these canons presuppose, the woman as a sexual being was excluded. Where such sexual dualism was predicated, man no longer defined himself in relation to woman . . . or expressed the conflict creatively; instead, he defined himself in separation from the woman.[12]

Laeuchli notes that the christian church still operates on the basis of this same antisexual dualism, which is, in effect, an antifemale dualism.[13] From the second century on, the church had portrayed sex as something pertaining to women and as evil, "the devil's gateway."[14] This attitude, for the first time, is canonized at the dawn of the era in which the church's social, political, and economic power is inaugurated.

The Elvira synod illustrates that a historical perspective on sexuality in western societies involves understanding the antisexual and antifemale (as well as anti-Semitic) character of christian teachings as a means of maintaining control in what was experienced as a chaotic social milieu, much like our own historical period.[15]

Understanding sexuality historically involves making connections between the social control of sexuality and the social control of women. Not only in christian history but moreover in western history (in which social control has been dominated by the church), the connection between women and sex has been so close as to be synonymous.

"The place of women in this chaotic world" is one of toil and trouble, scapegoating and violence, hatred and trivialization, poverty and despair.[16] Economically, under global structures of late capitalism, women are kept in poverty.[17] It is the way profit is maximized. Women's bodies are kept in the service of heterosexist patriarchy—as wives, whores, fantasy objects, and as a vast, deep pool of cheap labor.

We cannot comprehend the meaning of sexuality from a historical perspective without viewing its place in the context of power relations between genders. In particular, we must understand sexism, the oppression of women in which men are expected to play their manly roles—on top of women, enforcing the rules by which patriarchal, androcentric society is naturally and rightly ordered.

Behind the hostile slogan that "what a lesbian needs is a good fuck" is the less individualistic and more honest threat that what the society needs, in order to be well ordered, is for men to make women "enjoy" being dominated, held down, and screwed.

A historical reading of sexuality will teach us that sexual performance is often less a matter of enjoyment or pleasure—especially for women—than of necessity. Weeks writes of the modern movement for sexual liberation in the United States and Europe:

The sexual liberation of women was developing in a dual context: of male definitions of sexual need and pleasure, and of capitalist organisation of the labour market and of consumption (including consumption of sex in all of its many, frequently pornographic varieties). The junction of the two—(male definitions of sexual need and capitalist organization of labor) came through the material reality of family life. The economic position of most women—lower pay, fewer job opportunities—still ensures that marriage is seen as a gateway to financial as well as social security and position. And increasingly during this century, sex or at least sexual allure, has emerged as a guarantee for attaining status and security. We pay homage to an ideology of voluntarism in relation to marriage; the reality is often of an iron determinism, especially for women: economic, cultural, moral *and sexual*.[18]

For many women much of the time and some women all of the time, sex is not fun, it is not pleasurable, and yet it is what we are here to do—provide it for men. A historical understanding of sexuality demands that this reality be recognized.

Although western societies historically have been patriarchal and, on the whole, erotophobic, at no historical period have the links between sexual, gender, and economic control been more pernicious than today. Advanced capitalism literally feeds off of men's control of women's bodyselves, including the production of pornography, prostitution, rape, and other forms of sexual exploitation. Sex pays; and, in a culture of power-over social relations, coercive sex—involving pain and humiliation—pays best.

As a window into viewing our power in relation, a historical understanding of sexuality might help us begin to envision sex as erotic—the "life force" of the later Freud.[19] In his early writings, Freud linked sex and death. He never got fully away from this but he did begin to move away from his own theory. Building on the later Freud, Herbert Marcuse speaks of the "eroticization of the entire personality."[20] In so doing, he prefigures Audre Lorde's articulation of the erotic as the source of our creativity, the wellspring of our joy, the energy of our poems, music, lovemaking, dancing, meditation, friendships, and meaningful work.[21]

History, including the stories of our own lives and those of our forebears in relation, can teach us something about the erotic as creative power. The testimonies are there. Theologically, we are speaking of our power in right relation; from a christian perspective, the power of God.

Understanding sexuality historically might enable us also to experience sexual pleasure as good, morally right, without need of justification. Viewed through the traditional christian lens, this perception is scandalous—that our sensual, sexual pleasure is good, in and of itself, not merely as means to a good end.

In doing sexual ethics, we can refuse to play a defensive role. We do not need to justify pleasure. Let us rather have to justify pain—try to understand in what ways pain and suffering may be unavoidable, and sometimes necessary, in our lives. If we are to live with our feet on the ground, in touch with reality, we must help one another accept the fact that we who are christian are heirs to a body-despising, woman-fearing, sexually repressive religious tradition. If we are to continue as members of the church, we must challenge and transform it at the root. What is required is more than simply a "reformation." I am speaking of revolutionary transformation. Nothing less will do. [22]

Beverly Harrison, Dorothee Sölle, Margaret Huff, Janet Surrey, and other feminist liberation theologians and relational psychologists do not accept the concept of a personal "self" or "identity" apart from the relational matrix in which it is shaped. Theologically and ethically, our questions must include what it means for any of us to know her sexual "identity" in the relational praxis of transformation.

Language and change are a difficult fit. Words seem static, not fluid, which is why adjectives and transitive verbs tend to serve us better than nouns and intransitive verbs. And yet we must speak words as best we can. At no time has the urgency been more acute than today for us to share honest words about our bodyselves.

Our silence will not protect us. [23] Our best protection is to speak the truths of our lives insofar as we can, with one another's presence and help, and cultivate carefully together those truths we cannot yet speak, truths that may be still very unformed and young. We are shaping history with our words. Either we speak as best we can or our power in relation will slip away like a thief in the night.

Chapter 3

HETEROSEXISM: ENFORCING WHITE MALE SUPREMACY

In the dismembered world, we make love not to the living body of the Goddess but to her corpse. Power becomes sexualized. When all power is cast as domination, we can only feel our power through dominating another, and can give way only through our submission to another's control. The Master colonizes our orgasms.

—STARHAWK*

Growing up in an Irish Catholic family, sex was the ultimate forbidden subject. Ours was a family of silence and lies. Little was said out loud, only acted out and denied. . . . As the youngest of eight children . . . I did my best to live out the Christian and family virtues of servanthood, purity, silence, and obedience. . . .

In looking at my sexuality, I divide my lifeline into pre-Epiphany 1988 and post-Epiphany 1988. The word "epiphany" means sudden realization. The Epiphany is a Christian feast day celebrating the world's knowledge of the presence of Jesus Christ. It is also my birthday. I chose this significant day for my own personal epiphany. On January 6th of this year I walked into my therapist's office and announced that I wanted to discuss a previously taboo topic—my sexuality. I walked out with the knowledge that I was a victim of incest at my father's hands. . . .

My mind has painted layers of forgetfulness over memories of my father's unpredictable acts of violence toward me. It has only been a month since I first consciously realized that my father raped me. My tears can be triggered by anything or nothing these days, but my sexual responses

---

* Starhawk, *Truth or Dare: Encounters with Power, Authority, and Mystery* (San Francisco: Harper & Row, 1987), 204.

*are dead. I am protecting myself now as I was unable to
protect myself as a little girl. . . . I cannot look at my
sexuality without addressing how abuse has shaped it. Today my reaction to abuse is to shut down sexually.*

Monica,
theological student

Heterosexism is a foundational historical structure· of
our lives. Heterosexism is the social and political force named by
Adrienne Rich as the "institution of compulsory heterosexuality."
Rich describes how the "lie" of compulsory heterosexuality distorts women's lives in particular:

The lie of compulsory female heterosexuality today afflicts not just feminist
scholarship, but every profession, every reference work, every curriculum,
every organizing attempt, every relationship or conversation over which it
hovers. It creates, specifically, a profound falseness, hypocrisy, and hysteria
in the heterosexual dialogue, for every heterosexual relationship is lived in
the queasy strobe light of that lie. *However we choose to identify ourselves,
however we find ourselves labeled, it flickers across and distorts our lives.*
[My emphasis.]

The lie keeps numberless women psychologically trapped, trying to fit
mind, spirit, and sexuality into a prescribed script because they cannot
look beyond the parameters of the acceptable. It pulls on the energy of
such women even as it drains the energy of "closeted" lesbians—the energy
exhausted in the double-life. The lesbian trapped in the closet, the woman
imprisoned in prescriptive ideas of the "normal" share the pain of blocked
options, broken connections, lost access to self-definition freely and pow-
erfully assumed.[1]

Mario Mieli speaks in a similar fashion of "heterosexual ideology":

The repressive society only considers one type of *monosexuality* as "normal," the heterosexual kind, and imposes *educastration* with a view to
maintaining an exclusively heterosexual conditioning. The Norm, therefore, is heterosexual. [My emphasis.][2]

Heterosexism is the basic structure of gay/lesbian oppression in this and other societies. Heterosexism is to homophobia what sexism is to misogyny and what racism is to racial bigotry and hatred. Heterosexism is the *structure* in which are generated and cemented the *feelings* of fear and hatred toward queers and dykes, and toward ourselves if we are lesbians or gaymen. Dialectically, such feelings serve also to secure the structure. They thereby strengthen not only such traditional patriarchal religious institutions as christianity, which have helped set the structure of compulsory heterosexuality in place; but also more deeply personal "institutions," such as the self-loathing of homosexual youths and the hatred of such youths by others.

A "structure" is a pattern of relational transactions that gives a society its particular shape. Consider the analogy of a house. If there is a structural problem, we do not fix it by changing the wallpaper or rearranging the floor space. We cannot solve the structural problems of class elitism, racism, heterosexism, or any other "ism" by rearranging our institutions in such a way as simply to accommodate those who historically have been marginalized from the center of social, political, and economic power. To solve structural problems we must dig deeply into the foundations of our common life in order to discover the rot. Only then can we begin to reconstruct the house in such a way as to provide adequate, trustworthy space for us all.[3]

"Structure" denotes the interconnections between what may appear to be unrelated phenomena—such as the taking of foster children away from gay parents in Massachusetts; the granting of child custody to a heterosexually abusive father in Mississippi; the acquittal in Michigan of a nineteen-year-old man who admitted to raping his eight-year-old neighbor because she was "seductive"; the drowning of a young gay man in Bangor, Maine, by teenagers who thought he was "effeminate"; and the statement by a woman who, hearing of this murder, said, "Well, he probably made a pass at one of the boys." Heterosexism is a configuration of relational power in which such events are held together not merely as related but as critical parts of the whole configuration. Each event secures and reinforces the public educational impact of the others. This is how we learn to fear and hate others and ourselves.

Charlie Howard was not thrown off the bridge in Bangor simply because he happened to be an "effeminate" individual who had the misfortune of running into some particularly homophobic boys.[4] Charlie Howard was killed because all-American kids are taught by church, synagogue, and state to fear and hate fags. The three young men who killed Charlie Howard stand, in a representative sense, for the prevailing sexual moral ethos of our mainstream religions and our society. We cannot make the connections—between ecclesial traditions, homophobia, misogyny, and, in this case, murder—unless we see that no incident can be understood apart from the social structures that have shaped it. As an ugly act of wrong relation, gaybashing forces us to examine the structure of heterosexism as a *foundational resource of alienated power.*

In a profit-consumed economic order such as ours the value of persons is diminished. The accumulation of capital on the part of the wealthy and the hope for wealth on the part of the rest of us take precedence over the essentially nonmonetary value of human beings and other earthcreatures as valuable in our own right—because we are who we are. To claim we are valuable because "we are who we are" may, to our ears, sound "romantic" or "soft" or "simply a matter of faith." If so, we may have a clue of the depth of the cynicism that holds us collectively in its grip at this historical moment.

We humans, together with other earthcreatures, are diminished in the context of a late-twentieth-century capitalist global order. In this context, the capacity to love our bodies, enjoy a strong sense of self-esteem, take real pleasure in our work, and respect and enjoy either ourselves or others very much is a diminished capacity. In a very real sense, we have lost ourselves—that is, ourselves as a people, united with one another and other creatures.

This loss of ourselves and one another is what Marx meant by "alienation."⁵ In an alienated situation, we do not relate as humanely as we might desire. It is not that we may not want to be caring people. It is rather that, unbeknownst to us (usually to the extent that we hold power-over others in the society), we are captive to social forces that are running our lives. Most of us do not see the extent to which we are playing roles in society as if we had no choice. As individuals, to the extent that we are among the powerless, we do not have much "choice"—not if we want to live decently or, for many of us, if we want to survive (I'm referring here especially to poor people and people of color, and most especially to poor women of color).

For most United States citizens with access to survival resources, a preoccupation with "freedom" and its concommitant "privileges" of private ownership and private possession has its origins far beyond the realm of the individual's intention. All of us have received the message that the individual's freedom is our noblest possession, nobler than a quality of caring and dignity we might provide for one another. In the United States, among people of economic privilege, freedom is more important than justice. Whenever there must be a tradeoff, the freedom of the few will take precedence over justice for all.

Most of us learn that we should share what we have with others, especially the "less fortunate." But the dominant message in our civil and religious education is that the freedom of the individual must come first—especially for white propertied males. Men of color, all women, and the poor learn a similar lesson, but our capacities to achieve derive from our real or imagined relationships to white propertied males, whose right to set the agenda for the whole society has become a first principle of our civil religion.

In our alienated society, power has come to mean *power-over* others' lives, well-being, senses of self-worth, and survival. Power has come to mean domination by a few over the lives and deaths of many. I am referring to the real and daily domination of all human and other natural resources. The food we eat, the air we breathe, the energy we burn, the love we make, even the dreams we nurture, are controlled to a significant degree by the structural configurations of power that have been shaped by the interests of affluent white males who usually fail to see any more clearly than the rest of us the exploitative character of their own lives.

We and those with power over us have learned to assume that this alienation is natural. The state of being lost to ourselves and others is just the way it is and, in fact, must be if we are to preserve any portion of the social order we white folks tend to characterize as "free." In an alienated social order, it is necessary to be out of touch with the sacred value of that which is most fully human—common—among us. To be common is not a worthy aim for human beings who, in this situation, must strive to be "exceptional."

It's important that we recognize the extent to which an acceptance of this state of affairs as "just the way it is" characterizes contemporary United States society. Such massive resignation generates a sense of powerlessness, a collective depression, in which we lose our capacities for hope. For, while alienated power is not shared, alienated powerlessness is. It moves us slowly toward our undoing as a people on this planet.

To combat this sense of powerlessness, many people have organized against nuclear war, against the contras, against the so-called Right to Life movement, against racism. Yet it remains to this day unclear to many of us—at least those of us who are white middle-strata folk—what we are organizing *for*.

Alienated powerlessness is a social force that takes much of our most creative energy simply to withstand. It is easier to struggle *against* it than to generate fresh vision of a new and better social order. In an alienated situation, it's easier to be reactive than creative. The debilitating character of alienation creates reactionary progressives (such as the Democratic Party), a portent of pernicious things to come, as an entire society slips further away from the possibility of a common dream and a common good.

Audre Lorde's vision of the erotic as power is a creative social, emotional, spiritual, and political vision. Radically and simply, Lorde moves immediately into the heart of power as power-with, which for her is the erotic in our lives. In giving this deeply personal and political movement a voice, she speaks prophetically of who we can be together as we name and resist the structures of alienated power that keep us divided, separated, isolated, and depressed.

[The erotic]—that deep and irreplaceable knowledge of my capacity for joy—comes to demand from all of my life that it be lived within the knowledge that such satisfaction is possible, and does not have to be called *marriage*, nor *god*, nor an *afterlife*.

This is one reason why the erotic is so feared, and so often relegated to the bedroom alone, when it is recognized at all. For once we begin to feel deeply all the aspects of our lives, we begin to demand from ourselves and from our life-pursuits that they feel in accordance with that joy which we know ourselves to be capable of. Our erotic knowledge empowers us, becomes a lens through which we scrutinize all aspects of our existence, forcing us to evaluate those aspects honestly in terms of their relative meaning within our lives. And this is a grave responsibility, projected from within each of us, not to settle for the convenient, the shoddy, the conventionally expected, nor the merely safe.[6]

In sharp, violent opposition to this vision, alienated power is possessed, not shared. It is quantitative, not qualitative. Under advanced capitalism, alienated power is incarnated and symbolized by accumulation of wealth and property; manufacture, sale, and usage of guns and bombs; and the forcible thrusting of a penis into an unwanting vagina.

In this realm of greed and violence, more and bigger is best. We have it or we don't. It's natural to want it—for everyone to want wealth, for small countries to want bombs, and for women to want penises. In the moral ethos of the dominant social order, it is assumed that such power as capital, explosives, and rape can be used for either good or ill, depending on the purposes and judgment of those exercising it.

In this situation, no action is, in and of itself, evil—except that which challenges the established order of alienated power relations: So, for instance, while hunger may be a problem, communism, which threatens the individual white male's autonomy and his rights to private ownership, is evil. While wife-battering may be too bad, gay sex, which threatens the established order of male control of female sexuality, is evil. While incest may be a shame, lesbian mothers embody the forces of evil that threaten to bring down the entire sacred canopy of alienated power.

In its fullest sense, theologian James Nelson writes, our sexuality is "our way of being in the world as female or male persons. It involves our appropriation of characteristics socially defined as feminine or masculine. It includes our affectional-sexual orientation toward those of the opposite and/or same sex. It is our capacity for sensuousness."[7] Or, as Beverly Harrison suggests, it "deepens and shapes our power of personal being. Our sexuality represents our most intense interaction with the world. Because this is so, it is also a key to the quality and integrity of our overall spirituality."[8]

Our eroticism is the deepest stirring of our relationality, our experience of being connected to others. In the context of alienation, our eroticism, the root of our relational capacity, is infused with the experience of alienation. We are electrified by alienated power dynamics, turned on by currents of domination and submission that are structured into the world we inhabit. As mirrors of the world, our bodyselves reflect the violence intrinsic to the dynamics of alienated power. What we know, what we feel, and what we believe is mediated by images, symbols, and acts of domination and control.

We learn to associate survival—how we control our future, more basically, that we have a future—with symbols and acts of domination and violence. Whether at home, as is often the case, or elsewhere, children learn that whether or not might makes right, it shows who's in charge: a whipping by daddy, a war movie on television, a rock video about gang rape, a speech by the president about the so-called freedom fighters in Nicaragua. . . . These are paradigmatic lessons, unforgettable in the most embodied sense, by which we learn to experience our most personal world as fraught with the tension of being either more or less in control of our own daily lives.

We learn what is means to be child, parent, woman, man, dark, light, poor, rich, jew, christian, bad guy, good guy, bottom or top, down or up, less or more, powerless or power-more, vanquished or victorious. The dynamics of alienated power relations shape our sexualities as surely as they do the Pentagon budget.

Ours is a sadomasochistic society, quite literally, in that we have learned to sit back and enjoy the fruits of domination and submission. It is, for many of us, most of what we know to be relationally possible.

In the praxis of alienated power, the power of mutual relation is in eclipse. We have difficulty believing and immersing ourselves in the empowerment born of honest friendship. Relative to the overwhelming character of alienation, we are able to experience creative relational power primarily in glimpses, intimations, art, and—if we are lucky—in the sustaining of good friendship.

We may believe that the mutuality we experience in relation to some others is *good*, but we have not learned to trust it as *powerful*: the fulcrum of our capacity to survive and to affect the world around us.

We have come to assume, affectively if not cognitively, that while mutuality is playful and recreational, staying in control is the stuff of real creation. In this situation, mutuality doesn't seem to be an empowering relational dynamic, because in this context it isn't: *Mutuality does not breed alienated power. It transforms it.*

We have mastered our lessons as students of alienation: If we want to be successful, worthy women and men in this society, we must accept the fact that our power is generated by dynamics of control. We cannot allow ourselves to believe that the primary intensity and energy that emerges among friends and comrades gives us any serious control over our own lives. We learn to disbelieve in our most creative and redemptive power and become architects of our own isolation.

The sexual effects of disbelief in our relational power are staggering. So deluged are we by the romance of domination that most girls and boys, while they are still quite young, are well under the captivating spell of an eroticism steeped in fantasies of conquest, seduction, and rape. Such eroticism is "normal": that in which boy takes and girl is taken. Feminist theorists have demonstrated convincingly the extent to which "normal" human sexuality is synonymous with male gender domination. Any sexual desire or erotic stimulation that deviates from the normative status of male gender domination has been considered (until recently by the medical profession, and still by most mainline religions) to be "abnormal" or "wrong." While such abnormality includes homosexuality, it does not always include rape, especially "date rape," "marriage rape," or the forcible entry of a man's penis into the body of a woman or girl whom he knows (read: to whose body he has a "right").[9] As data mounts on the sexual violence perpetrated by men against women and girls, it becomes evident that rape, father-daughter incest, and other forms of sexual violence against women and children are considered, if not exactly "right," at least understandable and even tolerable by a shocking number of judges, therapists, and clergymen, who not infrequently are among the perpetrators.[10]

But we must watch carefully, because many of us experience the daily dynamics of domination and control most frequently as benign, not brutal; natural, not perverse. Abusive power can be difficult to detect, name, challenge, and expunge. Abusive dynamics, for example, are basic, even sacred, to traditional modes of parenting, religious leadership, physical, emotional, and spiritual healing, and teaching. In such relational transactions, movement in or toward mutuality is ruled out by those who, in the traditional arrangement, exercise power-over others.

The process of becoming more fully mutual cannot happen in

any relationship in which control must be maintained forever primarily by one party. Mutuality is impossible wherever the configuration of power is unchanging. In the praxis of alienation, this is how all significant relationships between individuals and groups have been structured.

It is vital, morally and spiritually, that we realize that we all participate in these fundamentally flawed relational dynamics of domination and submission. We can't escape them entirely without leaving the world. But we can help create a better way. To do so we need one another's friendship and solidarity. We must be patient, persevering, and tender with one another and ourselves. It will take years, decades, a long time, to learn, with one another, that our power to love is stronger than the fear that festers in our alienation.

Sexism is a structure of alienated power. It refers to the alienation between men and women, specifically to the historical complex of practices and attitudes that are essential to men's control of women's sexuality and, thereby, women's lives. *Heterosexism* is a logical and necessary extension of sexism. It is cemented in the false assumptions (1) that male gender superiority is good (natural, normal), and (2) that in order to secure sexism in the social order, men must be forced—if necessary—to control women's sexual activity.

Penetrating to the core of sexism, heterosexism heralds the recognition that, in order for women's sexual activity to be controlled, men's sexual activity must be imposed upon women. If women are to stay on the bottom of the male-female social relation, men must stay on top of women. In this way, men must be willing to do their part in preserving the structure of sexism. Otherwise, patriarchal, androcentric power relations will not prevail. Things will fall apart: romantic love between men and women, marriage and family as we know them, traditional values, the authority of traditional religious teachings, the stability of the social order, the security of the nation, everything predicated upon men's control of the world as we know it.

Heterosexist ideology is put in place to convince us that "normal" women are sexually submissive to men, and that "real" men sexually dominate women. Only when we understand heterosexism as the fundamental means of enforcing sexism and, therefore, as intrinsically bound up in the oppression of women, do we begin to understand why, historically, the gay/lesbian movement has come on the heels of the women's liberation movement. We begin also to see why feminists are clear that so-called women's issues and gay issues cannot be attended politically with any long-term effectiveness as long as their proponents attempt to keep them separate. The National Organization of Women in the early 1970s and the mainline protestant denominations have made this mistake. When we attempt not to confuse women's liberation with gay/lesbian liberation, we disregard deep organic connections between gender and sexual politics. In so doing, we subvert the possibility of any authentic gender or sexual transformation in our society and religious institutions.

Understanding the links between sexism and heterosexism may help illuminate also why so many openly self-affirming gaymen are feminists, and why so many frightened and ashamed homosexual men are not.[11] A gayman who understands the *sexist* character of his own oppression knows that those who govern the structures of patriarchal capitalism are determined to use his body to enforce the sexual control of women's lives. He is able to comprehend his homosexuality not simply as a private orientation or preference, but rather as a form of resistance to sexism, not necessarily chosen consciously, but a form of resistance nonetheless.

Those men, on the other hand, who experience their homosexuality as simply a private dimension of who they happen to be and what they happen to like fail generally to understand the feminist liberation commitment to making the connection between women's liberation and that of gaymen and others. Unable to make connections between their own private lives and the oppression of women, such homosexual men (whom the church always has gladly ordained) frequently are not merely indifferent to women's plight, but are hostile toward feminists and gaymen for having made sex-uality a matter of public interest, thereby threatening to invade their privacy.[12]

Homosexual people, like everyone else in heterosexist society, are homophobic. We are afraid of what our sexual involvement with members of the same sex may mean about us (that we are not "normal") or of what its consequences may be for us (forfeit of job, marriage, children, friends, ordination, and so on).

Our homophobia bears serious consequences for us. Many homosexual men and women are so terrorized by the meaning and potential consequences of their sexual orientation or preference that they cannot let themselves see the sexual politics of their own lives. Disempowered by fear, they fail to imagine the creative power inherent in struggling for justice and solidarity on behalf of the oppressed—including themselves.

Isolated, depressed, and cut off from the roots of their power in right relation, the wellspring of faith, these sisters and brothers do not yet believe that struggle is a name for hope.[13] But our lives are linked with theirs, and we should remember to make room for them at the table whenever they are able to come forth.

Chapter 4

A SACRED CONTEMPT:
HETEROSEXIST THEOLOGY[1]

The liberation of God is not simply a matter of changing the way we talk about God. God himself and not just human language must be liberated.

—CAROL CHRIST*

I was raised in the Roman Catholic church. I am of Irish descent. I was educated for the most part in parochial schools. . . . As a result of my religious training, my attitudes toward sex were negative. Sex meant "doing it." And "doing it" was for marriage and childbearing. Beyond that, sex/sexuality did not play a meaningful part in my life. It was, it seemed, a necessary evil. A very strong emphasis in my training was that it was the girl's/woman's responsibility to see that nothing "happened." We were to speak, dress, act in such a way as not to "excite" the boys. They could not be held responsible for their sexual feelings. "Boys will be boys."

The human body was to be respected as "the temple of the Holy Spirit." It was to be cared for as one might take care of a car or other machine so that it would function well as a transportation vehicle of the "spirit." It was not good or to be enjoyed in and of itself. Its proclivity toward sensuality had to be constantly checked.

Eleanor,
theological student

Heterosexist theology is constructed on the assumption that male domination of female lives is compatible with the will

---

* Carol Christ, *Laughter of Aphrodite: Reflections on a Journey to the Goddess* (San Francisco: Harper & Row, 1987), 20.

of God. The rightness of compulsory heterosexuality is predicated on the belief that in a natural order, heterosexuality alone is good. Any deviation from it is sinful. Basing contemporary moral theory on medieval concepts of natural law necessitates projecting an image or fantasy of "good order" onto human social relations—thereby denying altogether the role of human agency in determining moral good.[2] We play no part in creating sexual morality.

While belief in natural law may not strike us as necessarily heterosexist, in a sexist situation like the praxis of the church, the assumption of a natural order is infused with the corollary presuppositions about gender and sexuality.[3] In this social praxis, historical and contemporary, the image of heterosexual marriage emerges as the prototype for the Right—that is, the Natural and Moral—Relation not only between male and female, but also between Christ and his church. Compulsory heterosexuality safeguards this divinely willed Right Relation. To coerce heterosexual bonding is simply to affirm what is natural. And what is natural reflects the good order of the cosmos, thereby revealing the divine purpose. The Be-ing of God involves being heterosexual.

The church often draws on individualistic psychology for support in upholding the sanctity of compulsory heterosexual relations. Church bodies often commission psychiatrists to make clinical judgments of individual candidates for the ordained ministry. More often than not, the person's health is understood by the ecclesiastical authority (and often by the psychiatrist) as synonymous with being heterosexual and married (or open to marriage)—or, at least, with the candidate's willingness to abstain from sexual activity outside marriage. On this basis, church authorities frequently will deny that they are against homosexuality per se, but rather will insist that they are opposed to all sexual activity outside of marriage, heterosexual as well as homosexual. To the rejoinder that *homosexual* marriages are not permitted in church, the typical response is bewilderment, as if the very notion were unintelligible to christian sensibilities of what is both natural and moral.[4]

It should not be surprising that the church would consecrate psychology as its Great High Priest. Psychology, for the most part, remains the most highly individualistic of the modern sciences, and liberals have strong investment in the interior life and yearnings of individuals as the locus of sin and grace, problems and transformation.[5] Moreover, what is psychologically "normal" provides the content for the theologian's understanding of what is natural and moral. What specifically is lacking in most psychology, as in most theology, is a critical analysis of the ways in which unjust power relations between men and women shape the lens through which we view the natural/moral order. Liberal proponents of natural law fail to enter into serious engagement with those whose lives are marginalized by its truth-claims.

Liberal christianity is morally bankrupt in relation to women and homosexuals. The liberal church damages us because, as a theopolitical ideology, liberalism not only is set against collective advocacy as a primary mode of christian witness; it is also contemptuous of the particular claims of feminists and openly gay-men and lesbians.

Paul Tillich was a paradigmatic modern liberal. His theology portrays an amoral, individualistic God-Man as constitutive of Being itself. His widow, Hannah, tells of a conversation between "the old woman and the old man":

"Why do you always remain on the borderline?" asked the old woman. "Why can't you decide between Yin and Yang, between the mountains and the deep blue sea? . . ."
"Why should I decide?" retorted the old man nastily. "I don't know where I belong. Besides, indecision allows for freedom."[6]

Tillich went beyond the romantic reductionism of natural law into a more complex theological reasoning that took some account of the ambiguities of human existence. Still, his theology suffered from problems classic to liberal philosophy. First, he did not have an adequate understanding of the social, relational basis of either human or divine Being. "Being" was, for Tillich, constitutive of the inner life of the individual agent. Second, for this reason, Tillich did not see the *theological* significance of the material, embodied, and economic grounds of human being. His specific focus was on the ability of the well-educated Euroamerican male to cope spiritually within the "structures of existence." His concept of God, a logical companion piece to his anthropology, floats free of the contingencies of relationality, physicality, and material need—and thus from our actual "ground of being."[7]

Tillich recognized his own "estrangement" as constitutive of his "existence." He noted a problem with the extent to which christian theologians traditionally have rendered estrangement—or sin—as rooted in "concupiscence," or sexual desire. Of the church's "ambiguous" attitude toward sex, Tillich wrote, "The church has never been able to deal adequately with this central ethical and religious problem."[8]

Tillich seemed puzzled by this lingering devaluation of sex in christian tradition. He evidently did not notice a connection in christian history between the devaluation of sex and the devaluation of women. This oversight reflects the bias in Tillich's perspective on the meaning of estrangement, creation, existence, and essence. His worldview, grounded in his experience and articulated in his theology, revealed much about the "actualized creation and estranged existence" of someone who failed to acknowledge (or perhaps even to notice) that the limits of his theological epistemology were set not only by his "finitude" as "man," but more particularly by his experience as one white German male academic.

Writing on behalf of all men (more honestly, all white academic christian men struggling with *angst*), Tillich subsumed the conditions of human existence under a series of ontological polarities: Every man lives in tension between the *angst* of his existence and the divine essence from which he has fallen into this alienated situation. Tillich's fundamental image of human life reflected his experience of existing between death/dying and life/living.

Tillich's academic concern was not essentially a moral one, and he did not reduce death to evil or life to good. Nonetheless, his theology suggested that human existence is synonymous with a moral struggle with Nonbeing and that, in the struggle, justice is actualized as a moral good. Still, this existential process is located in the life of the individual man.[9]

Feminist ethicist Norene M. Carter has suggested that since Tillich failed to present alienation as a social, material condition, his ontology did not address adequately the moral issues involved in human alienation from other humans, the rest of creation, or the Creator.[10] Human *angst* originates not in the individual's psycho-spiritual ontology but rather in the historical structures of alienated social relations, which render each person victor or vanquished in a myriad of relational configurations that are beyond her or his individual capacity to alter.

To those who cannot accept the traditional God of theism, Tillich offered the image of a "God above God" who is eternally beyond the structures of existence.[11] It is from this God above God that we have fallen into alienated existence. And it is with this God that we can reunite in New Being, through participation and transformation by Christ, the Essential God-Man.[12] In refusing to confuse essence with existence, God with man—even in Christ— Tillich misleads us, drawing us away from realizing the part we may play in the drama of salvation.

Tillich did not deny the importance of human "acceptance" of the New Being.[13] He also did not stress, however, the role of human agency in salvation. This is probably because he did not recognize the corporate character of being—either human or divine—and thus was struck epistemologically and soteriologically in his perception that "man" (the individual white male) must be "grasped" by an ontological force (New Being, or the Christ) outside himself before he can participate in the drama of salvation.

Ironically, while Tillich was attempting to present a theology to cut through the lonely individualism of human existence, he failed to grasp the creative power of human subjectivity when "humanity" is understood as an *essentially corporate reality:*

The objective reality of the New Being precedes subjective participation in it. . . . Regeneration (and conversion), understood this way, have little in common with the attempt to create emotional reactions in appealing to an individual in his subjectivity.[14]

Tillich drew us beyond the structures of our existence, however dehumanizing and oppressive, toward an "essence" that should not be confused with our daily human experiences of love and work, pain and struggle, confusion and play. But does it suffice to suggest that our alienation originates in our fall from God, in the spiritual malaise of individual men and women? It may be small comfort to imagine that the solution to our predicament is to bear up courageously on the basis of whatever mental gymnastics enable us to leap high enough or probe deep enough to be grasped by New Being.

Despite his insistence that it is entirely at the initiative of the "divine Spirit" that "man" is "grasped" by the "New Being," the bulk of Tillich's work reflected his efforts to seek, find, and be open to the "essential God-man."[15] Again, the problem is that Tillich did not acknowledge the collective, relational, sensual, and embodied ground on which he stood with others, a "ground of being" on which justicemaking has more to do with one's acceptance of social, relational responsibility than with one's actualization of "as many potentialities as possible without losing oneself in disruption and chaos."[16]

Tillich took little account of the social, political, and historical character of each individual, thus little account of the limits of the individual's spiritual aspirations. *Neither Tillich nor other liberal christians comprehend deeply creative power, at once human and divine, as historically and ontologically embodied among us, transacted between and among ourselves daily as cocreative agents upon whom the power of love in history depends.*

The liberal deity, in some anthropomorphic sense, may "love" us; but it is likely to tax our understandings of what actual loving involves. A God above God (or an Essential God-Man) remains eternally unaffected by the clamor and clutter of human struggle, including the passions, problems, and confusions of human sexuality.

On the surface, Tillich's theology has *nothing* to do with sexism, heterosexism, racism, or any other ism. That is precisely the point of liberal philosophy: God is simply above the fray. This, more than any other, is the grievance of Latin American, African American, Asian American, and feminist liberation theologians against the so-called objectivity espoused by liberal theological scholars. This "objectivity" presupposes the subject's ability to manufacture a critical distance between himself and his object of study (such as "God") in order to produce a theology free of bias or ideology.

A more perceptive hermeneutic suggests that Tillich's theology, his portrait of God, has everything to do with holding traditional power arrangements in place. For his God above God is finally indifferent to the details of how we live together on the earth. The Prince of Wales and the prisoner on death row, the murdered gay activist Harvey Milk and his murderer Dan White, have the same ontological constitution and live under the same conditions of existence. Their salvation histories involve, essentially, the same *angst. Because liberalism has no adequate power analysis, a liberal disposition fails to notice its own moral bankruptcy.*

The traditional God/Father's anthropomorphic antagonism toward women and wanton sexual behavior is well documented in christian history. Unlike this God, the liberal God of self-consciousness, human potential, therapy, and science controls women and homosexual people not because he is hostile to us (God forbid!), but rather because he is neutral in relation to us.

Liberal morality is generated in an individualistic realm, in which the subject determines right from wrong. As Friedrich Schleiermacher wrote,

But in the sinful nature the bad exists only correlatively with the good, and no moment is occupied exclusively by sin. . . . Insofar as the consciousness of our sin is a true element of our being, *and sin therefore a reality*, it is ordained by God as that which makes redemption necessary. [My italics.][17]

Not only are good and evil, grace and sin, necessary correlates in the work of redemption in liberal protestantism, but the reality of sin is predicated upon our noticing it! We are first and finally moral monads, accountable to the pangs of our own God-*consciousness*, not to a God whose justice may be calling us to account *regardless* of how we may feel about it or what we may think.

Among liberals, one simply holds one opinion while someone else holds another. No judgment is passed. What may be at stake morally goes unnoticed when there is no understanding of how our power relations shape our opinions. Liberal priests, therapists, and others fail to recognize fully the significance of the power they hold over others. They do not see the demonic character of unequal power relations nor do they see the sacred character of mutual power relations.

Liberals do not understand the term *power relations* as denoting the dynamic context in which our lives constantly are being shaped by, and are shaping, one another's. From a liberal perspective, *power* is either a social force or established authority that belongs to someone or it is a personal charisma anyone can receive. In a liberal worldview, power is not understood as pertaining to how we live in the ongoing tensions between creativity and destruction, life-enhancing and death-dealing dynamics, solidarity and alienation, healing and abuse, which affect us all.

To believe that we can discern our own ethics, choose from many options, and act on the basis of individual "conscience" is to admit defeat in the struggle against the structures of our alienation. It is to give *explicit* assent to the immoral proposition that whether one rapes or not, pays taxes or not, drops the bomb or not, are decisions that only the responsible individual or individuals can make. It is furthermore to give implicit assent to the dualistic assumption that such matters, in historical fact, are none of God's business. In the realm of God, the opinions of a Jesse Helms and a Jesse Jackson are of equal consequence—none at all. For the liberal deity has turned over to us the realm of human affairs. What we do, each of us, about racism, sexism, heterosexism, or any other human problem is our business.

To their peril, many women as well as homosexual christians draw upon the moral neutrality of christian liberalism in arguing for their right to live and let live.[18] This is a self-defeating argument, for the problems of injustice cannot be solved by appeals to "freedom" and "differences of opinion" as value-free "rights."[19] From a moral perspective, freedom is not value free. It is the power of personal agency in the context of *just* social relations in which the positive value of all persons has been established as a given.

Of course, it would seem logical that, pleading for neutrality and freedom in matters of morality, liberal christians should have no reason to believe that God cares whether people are feminists, lesbians, or gaymen. It would seem truer to its own ethical heritage if the liberal church were to say to its members who do not conform to traditional gender roles or sexual practices: "God doesn't care whether you are gay or straight, or whether you are a feminist or an adherent to traditional gender roles. God wants you to be true to yourself and faithful in relation to God and God's people." But this is not what most liberal churches have said.

In one sense, the implications of theological liberalism for gaymen, lesbians, and feminists are identical with those for all women, racial/ethnic minority peoples, the poor, and others whose oppression should be of more immediate moral concern to church leaders than the "spiritual" pilgrimages of individuals.

There is another sense, however, in which gender and sexual injustice occupy a special place at the hallowed table of christian fellowship. Sexism and heterosexism receive a particular "blessing" from the liberal philosophical tradition's *trivialization* of the female gender and human sexuality as embodied, material, "lower" phenomena. The "normative dualism" of christian liberalism has been shaped by sexism and sealed in heterosexism.[20]

I need not elaborate here examples from the works of christian fathers who have located creative spiritual power in the hypothetically disembodied male mind.[21] Thus today, while the material concerns of *men* of color and poor *men* can be subsumed *idealistically* into the liberal vision of a nonracist, nonclassist world, women and openly homosexual people *embody and represent* the specific material phenomena that, in christian idealism, came early to its full expression in the contributions of Augustine.

From the standpoint of christian idealism, to press seriously for women's liberation or for the affirmation of gay and lesbian sexual activity is to fly in the face of the idealistic tradition, in which femaleness and sexual activity are, *de facto*, ungodly and thus singularly undeserving of the justice that constitutes the liberal vision of the divinely ordained world.[22] Thus does liberal christianity embody its own contradiction between its ideal of one, inclusive world and its sacred contempt for femaleness and sexual passion.[23]

While many liberal churches appear to have attended to the problem of sexism, they fail utterly to take heterosexism seriously and thus actually fail to do justice to women's lives, whether lesbian, heterosexual, bisexual, genitally active, genitally inactive, or celibate.

The liberal churches have always displayed some measure of tolerance toward those women and homosexual people whose *public* presence has been strictly in conformity with patriarchal social relations.[24] Passive, self-effacing women, and men and women who have kept their homosexual activities closeted from public knowledge, have been well received, on the whole, throughout christian history. Such women and men have comprised a large part of the church. Women and homosexual people pose no practical problem to the church unless we *publicly challenge* the church's sexism and heterosexism.

This is exactly what is happening today. Many feminists, gaymen, and lesbians have begun to come out of our concealment and put ourselves visibly on the ecclesial line as representative of those women and men who, throughout christian history and the ecumenical church today, have seen that the liberal christian emperor has no clothes—no sense of the misogynist, erotophobic, and oppressive character of his realm.

Thus it is true that, from the standpoint of advanced patriarchal capitalist social relations, the liberal deity has begun to incorporate, superficially, the "rights" of women and of racial/ethnic minorities and the poor into his divine agenda as *idealistic* moral claims that need not disrupt the harmony of life as it is meant to be lived in the realm of God. However, the feminist and gay/lesbian demand (not request) that women and homosexual persons be affirmed (not tolerated) poses a challenge not only to the good ordering of liberal social relations, but also a threat to the essence of liberal religion. For the liberal deity is, above all, a noncontroversial gentleman— the antithesis of much that is embodied by feminists and by openly gaymen and lesbians who dare to challenge the moral deficit of liberal christianity. At stake, finally, from a feminist liberation perspective, are not the bodies of witches and faggots, but the nature and destiny of God.

Chapter 5

AUTHORITY AND SCRIPTURE: THAT WHICH CAN BE TRUSTED

To trust in heart, in erotic power, is a dangerous act.
— RITA NAKASHIMA BROCK[*]

My coming out as a lesbian six years ago was both assisted and handicapped by the Roman Catholic tradition in which I was raised. . . . My mother tells a story in which she discovered me in the closet with the door shut when I was five. When she asked what I was doing in there, I told her I was talking to God. . . . My faith is very personal, empowering, but demanding. God helped me to cope with the isolation I felt as a "baby dyke" in a very straight, very scary world. I thought for a while that I might join a religious community of women, but the demands of celibacy and the inherent second-class status of women religious in the church turned me off that idea. This faith carried me through high school and college, even into a sexual relationship with a woman, which was plagued by confusion and guilt (we used to pledge to give up sex for Lent—a doomed effort). Gradually the incongruence between my feelings and the expectations of the church, my family, society, and my own internalized homophobia began to crumble my closet. . . .

So I came screaming out of the closet. Coming out overturned my theological assumptions and, therefore, my assumptions about justice, relationship, what is normal, what is right relationship, who is Jesus to me, what is redemption, etc. I escaped the Catholic church. I left as

---

[*] Rita Nakashima Brock, *Journeys By Heart: A Christology of Erotic Power* (New York: Crossroad, 1988), 107.

> *a battered woman leaves her batterer—frightened, with no-*
> *where to go, unclear of what good, if any, lies ahead. But*
> *I left to survive.*
>
> Janet,
> theological student

I begin with a story about authority, which I heard many years ago:

Once there was a wise old woman, a witch, who lived in a small village. The children of the village were puzzled by her—her wisdom, her gentleness, her strength, and her magic. One day several of the children decided to fool the old woman. They believed that no one could be as wise as everyone said she was, and they were determined to prove it. So the children found a baby bird and one of the little boys cupped it in his hands and said to his playmates, "We'll ask her whether the bird I have in my hands is dead or alive. If she says it's dead, I'll open my hands and let it fly away. If she says it's alive, I'll crush it in my hands and she'll see that it's dead." And the children went to the old witch and presented her with this puzzle. "Old woman," the little boy asked, "This bird in my hands— is it dead or alive?" The old woman became very still, studied the boy's hands, and then looked carefully into his eyes. "It's in your hands," she said."[1]

Genuinely creative authority, sacred at its root, is in our hands. It moves us more fully into our bodyselves-in-relation. It touches and often frightens us as it calls us forth to become more fully who we are already: interdependent and mutual participants in this journey we call life.

The word "authority" comes from the Latin verb *augere*, which means to cause to grow, to augment that which already is. Deriving from *augere*, the Latin *auctor* (author) means one who creates or brings into being. Jesuit theologian Avery Dulles defines authority as "that which (or those whom) one has reason to trust."[2]

In this spirit, I offer a definition of authority as that which calls into being "something" that is already and, for that reason, can be trusted. The reason we can trust the authority of the story or re-source or person is that it does not impose an extraneous set of expectations upon us but rather evokes "something" we already know, or have, or are. We need authority precisely for the purpose of helping us discover, recover, empower, and encourage ourselves and one another.

This experience of authority as organic and encouraging to who we are at our best is the antithesis of the more prevalent notions—and experiences—of authority as "force," "coercion," or "violence." In the dominant culture, the imposition of will and judgment by those with power-over has become synonymous with authority. But, as social philosopher Hannah Arendt taught, if it's coercive, it's not authority: not *real* authority, not that which touches us in our souls, the foundational "place" within us in which we meet one another and find ourselves at home.[3]

Force serves always to diminish. That is the purpose of violence. People who have to make us do something through rules, punish-ment, threats, or intimidation may exercise force in our lives, but they hold no real authority for us. Because authority is that which (or those whom) we can trust to help us become more, not less, ourselves.

No person, religion, tradition, profession, rule, or resource should be inherently authoritative for us. We should always ask this question: Does it help us realize more fundamentally our con-nectedness to one another and hence the shape of our own iden-tities as persons-in-relation?

The authority that can be trusted calls forth something that al-ready is—and, if the authority is sacred, the "something" is the possibility of mutuality. When we speak with such authority, or are touched by the authority of others as a resource of blessing, it is because they and we are relating in such a way as to call forth who we are in right relation.

The value and meaning of authority, in the praxis of mutual relation, is to shape justice, the logos of God. As such, authority is the power to elicit among us, between us, and within us that which already is, to give birth to who we are when we are related rightly. The authority of God is not the power to create out of nothing (the mythos of patriarchal deity), but rather the power to cocreate out of the fabric of our daily lives who we are when we are related mutually—with justice and compassion.

Ecclesiastical, civil, or professional laws and rules hold genuine authority in our lives only insofar as we experience them as forged in our actual struggles toward right relation. To be creative rather than coercive, real and not rhetorical, authority must be shaped in the context of our movement into mutually empowering relationship. This relational dynamic is the heartbeat of God, her purpose and her passion.

The struggle for mutuality is what my former colleague and process theologian John E. Skinner might call the *arche*, or beginning point, of authority.[4] We need an *arche*—an initial reason—for authority if we are to understand and experience it as redemptive rather than as coercive and damaging. In his work, Skinner cites Hannah Arendt's perception that authority has disappeared in our time because we have lost "the primordial sources" for it—sources such as faith in God; belief in the inerrancy (or at least primacy) of the bible as the Word of God; confidence in the nation and in such civil religious institutions as marriage, monogamy, and the United States presidency.[5]

Might the struggle for the possibility of relational mutuality be a primordial source for our authority? Might we come to experience and understand this struggle as the *arche* of authority in our lives— an authority that is neither simply outside us nor inside us, but rather is generated between and among us?

That which we can trust meets us in the relation between and among ourselves. No one of us "has" it. Authority is not a possession. It is our *dunamis:* dynamic, relational power.[6]

In relation to "fallen" humanity, the church historically has taught a doctrine of external authority: God not only is not us; he is not like us. Divinity is, in fact, the very antithesis of humanity. In relation to this absolute authority, we are "ungodly," we earth-creatures, especially we human creatures with frightful psychospiritual parts called "wills," by which we "sin." Only "in Christ" are we saved *from ourselves*—that is, from the consequences of our sin, which are themselves the consequences of our having wills, or minds of our own. Moral and spiritual authority must come from beyond us sinners.

The enlightenment brought a major shift in the spiritual consciousness of western society. Increasingly secular over the last three hundred years, western man (white male with access to economic privilege) has been custodian of authority. With idealistic goals of autonomy, individuality, and independence, this man assumes that he has a right to do pretty much as he pleases. There are limits, but they are few, and they are all constructed by way of upholding his rights. His right to swing his fist stops at someone else's nose; otherwise, he may swing away.

Moving beyond the authoritative aegis of organized religion, this man's authority is, supposedly, internal. Whatever may be right or true, for himself (and, by extension, for others as well) becomes known to him through his reason, goodwill, and self-control.

This understanding of "man" as master of his own destiny undergirds the prevailing civil religion of the United States, hence also the established institutions of our lives such as government, business, family, religion, education, medicine, and law. The good order of these institutions often is secured in such forms of internal authority as honor systems; respect for conscience; and placing a high value upon virtues of reason, mental stability, and personal reputation.

Such a self-possessed man is able to choose freely to be in relation with others. In his life, there is no place for external authority except that which safeguards his autonomy—his right, that is, to be his own internal authority. This is, for example, why we must have a "strong defense against communism," to protect the freedom of the free white male and his female or "colored" clones to be their own authorities. This is the climate in which the republican party proudly glories and that the Dukakis-Bentsen democrats failed in 1988 to challenge as morally bankrupt.

The christian bible, like any resource, may become a spiritual license to build the world in the image of one's own self. This tendency to present "the word of God" as one's own agenda—myopic and nonrelational—is commonplace among those who hold civil and ecclesial power. It has been happening rather dramatically for the past decade in the United States.

As an instrument wielded to hold the power in place, the bible has been used recently to *confirm* the broken, isolated, frightened dimensions of our human experience. Religious and secular leaders have used the bible to call forth the worst in us—that is, to evoke the illusion that we are, in fact, separate, autonomous characters, helpless and powerless as a people. To a large extent, we who are christians have internalized this message and, as such, believe ourselves to be living daily on the basis of an internal authority ("reason" or "faith," for example), which has taught us that we can do little, if anything, to change the established order of power relations.

In this way, a doctrine of internal authority has free rein among us today—provided that we locate and accept our own interests as compatible with those of white, ostensibly heterosexual, affluent christian males. Upon others—marginalized people, sexual deviants, and political dissidents, for example—external authority characteristically is brought to bear in forms of force and punishment.

From a feminist liberation theological and ethical perspective, both external and internal notions of authority are inadequate. Neither is born in, nor gives birth to, mutuality as a vital life-force that is the substance of love, friendship, and voluntary cooperation at all levels of human engagement.

When Arendt suggests that authority has disappeared because the primordial sources for it are lost, she is not lamenting the loss of simplistic authoritarian solutions. She is stating simply what she perceives to be true: that, in the mid- (now late-) twentieth century, we westerners have lost our footing. We don't have anything to believe in, and we are looking in all the wrong places and directions.

Dorothee Sölle, in her first book, written as an essay on "The 'Death of God,' " proposes that the problem with modern humanity is that we've lost our identity, collectively and individually.[7] She focuses on "identity" rather than "authority" in this work, but the two are closely related. Not surprisingly, Sölle moves to a biting critique of "obedience" in her next book.[8] Like Dietrich Bonhoeffer, Sölle contends that we westerners, christians in particular, are lost, without either a *deus ex machina*—a mechanical, externalized authority—or a clear internal sense of what difference any of us can make in a world that has produced the Holocaust and the Vietnam war.

Over the last twenty years, Sölle has emerged as one of the leading proponents in western christianity of a radically relational ethic in which what we do enhances the well-being of the whole inhabited earth—or else damages it.

For Sölle, God is both the *act* of justicemaking/lovemaking and *those* who struggle for justice for themselves and others.[9] God is both active and personal, movement and faces. Similarly, our authority is secured both in the *struggle* to love and as the *resting place* among lovers and beloveds.

There is no religious institution or sacred text that is the Authority for Dorothee Sölle. God is authority, but God is never, for Sölle, simply the mirror image of her own psyche or will. God is literally the creative, liberating power that moves the global struggles for justice, as well as the spark in our own efforts to befriend one another in this world. Dorothee Sölle, as much as anyone, has been authoritative in my own emerging sense that authority, to be moral, must be relational, open, changing, and rooted constantly in our struggles for justice, friendship, compassion, and joy.

What might be a relational definition of *scripture?* Scripture, or sacred writings, is a broader concept than the bible. Most christians are likely either not to know this or to forget it. All major religions have their scriptures. Only christianity has the bible, though jewish scripture includes what christians historically have called the "Old Testament" or, more recently, "Hebrew Scriptures," referring to the language of the documents rather than to their relation, from a christian perspective, to the "New Testament." While the bible is a fixed set of books, a "canon"—meaning "rule" or "standard"— which was closed in the fourth century C.E., scripture refers more generally to the body of primary resources of a religious tradition.

Let's examine briefly the role of the christian bible as scripture. While for most christians the bible and holy scripture are synonymous, catholic and protestant emphases on scriptural (biblical) authority have been different. The catholic tendency (roman, orthodox, and anglo-) has been to subsume biblical authority under the vast authoritative rubric of "tradition", while the protestant bias has been to grant the bible a singular place of authority in determining what the church should teach.[10]

The anglican *via media* has been an effort not to combine catholicism and protestantism per se, but rather to sustain creative tension in the midst of different authoritative resources—scripture, tradition, and reason.

Arguing against the Puritan claim that the bible is the only source of revelation and hence should be sole authority for christians, anglican Richard Hooker (b. 1600) wrote,

Some things [wisdom] openeth by the sacred books of Scripture; some things by the glorious works of Nature: with some things she inspireth them from above by spiritual influence; in some things she leadeth and traineth them only by worldly experience and practice. We may not so in any one special kind admire her, that we disgrace her in any other, but let all her ways be according unto their place and degree adored.[11]

On behalf of reason, he continued,

We have endeavored to make it appear, how in the nature of reason itself there is no impediment, but that the selfsame spirit, which revealeth the things that God hath set down in his law, may also be thought to aid and direct men in finding out by the light of reason what laws are expedient to be made for the guiding of his Church, over and besides them that are in Scripture.[12]

In a word, the anglican position on the authority of the bible can be interpreted as relational: We are to draw upon biblical authority in relation to the rest of our faith-heritage (tradition) as well as our own best judgment (reason) in living responsibly in our own generation. The bible does not, and cannot, stand alone: not for anglicans.

While anglican (or episcopal) candidates for ordination must take an oath declaring that we believe "the Old and New Testaments to be the Word of God and to contain all things necessary to salvation," our religious tradition has never presupposed that the bible stands alone as God's word, nor that it is the only sacred resource that contains "all things necessary to salvation," nor that everything it contains is necessary to salvation. Or so we who are progressive anglicans continue to teach one another.

The fact is, much in the buoyant, idealistic spirit of anglicanism, I am idealizing my religious tradition as I write. I should go no further without acknowledging that, like other christians, both catholic and protestant, most anglicans use the bible as authoritative insofar as it justifies our purposes.

We may have been masters seeking to keep our slaves or to free our slaves; we may have been slaves seeking our freedom or making peace with our oppression. Christians have used the bible to support a wide variety of morally disparate efforts, and to sustain us in our morally diverse ways of living. We who are christians still do—be we episcopalians, roman catholics, or baptists; radicals, liberals, or evangelicals; lesbians and gaymen or fundamentalists who believe that homosexuals are doomed to hell. We use the bible to support our own purposes.

The selective use of biblical teachings does not have to be dishonest or damaging to ourselves or others. Usually, however, it is. Using the bible as if we ourselves were divinely ordained custodians of the Truth bears serious consequences, usually for others. This happens because we fail to see or acknowledge, in citing the bible, that we are speaking our own values, our own words, in what we believe to be faithful relation to the bible. In this way, we easily resort to making pious assumptions about the authority of "the Word of God," as if a great patriarchal Father had given us personally a piece of his mind to market for him.

Only a patriarchal deity, constructed in the minds of men who have been out of touch with one another and themselves, would be so arrogant as to assume that his Word is *the* Word or that, on such exclusivistic terms, it can be marketed morally. And only a spiritually vacuous imagination would have dreamt up such a god. But, to a troubling degree, this is the christian legacy.

Can we dream beyond these dreams of men who have created, in their lonely, dispassionate images, the Master of the entire universe, including each of our isolated, fragmented selves? Only insofar as we are moving together beyond this spiritual narcissism, which has brought western civilization (and with it the world) close to the brink, can we read and hear the christian bible as *a* word of God.[13] For, when interpreted by our lives-in-relation as a word of love, the bible is a word of God. Like the Upanishads, Bhagavad Gita, Torah, Koran, and scriptures of other major patriarchal religious traditions, the bible can be a resource for liberation if it inspires us to envision and embody justice and to resist domination, subordination, violence, and greed. The bible is not a word of God when it is used to justify structures and dynamics of unjust power relations.

In movements for abolition of slavery and for civil rights; for gender, sexual, racial, and economic justice; for food, health care, jobs, and decent wages; for human dignity, compassion, and respect for the earth, the bible is interpreted every day in every generation as a word of liberation, sacred speech, a word of God.

In service, however, of racial hatred and discrimination, economic exploitation, sexual, gender, and other forms of injustice, christian imperialism and other forms of domination, the bible not only is not sacred speech, it is perverse—turned around completely from the possibility of being shared as a resource of love and liberation, a word of God. Unfortunately, the bible is used at least as often in the service of evil as it is on behalf of justicemaking and lovemaking among and between us. Upholding injustice, the bible becomes a primary resource of fear, sin, hatred, and oppression.

How then can we be certain that we who are christians are using the bible in the work of liberation? Let's ask this question in another way: On what basis, for christians, is the bible part of our sacred scripture? On what basis is the bible a resource of authority for us as people who need that which can be trusted to call us, a day at a time, more fully into right, mutual relation among ourselves and with the rest of the whole inhabited earth?

Departing the company of most other christian feminist exegetes and interpreters, New Testament scholar Elisabeth Schüssler-Fiorenza contends that the bible does not hold intrinsically its own liberating impulse or theme, such as a "prophetic core," which allows it to establish its own norm in the work of justice:

Rather than seek a "revealed" Archimedean point in the shifting sand of biblical-historical relativity—be it a liberating tradition, text, or principle in the Bible—a feminist critical hermeneutics has to explore and assess whether and how Scripture can become an enabling, motivating resource and empowering authority in women's struggle for justice, liberation, and solidarity.[14]

I agree with Schüssler-Fiorenza that the bible is not, therefore, a "sacred text" in the traditional sense of being able to stand by itself, immune from critical accountability to the tasks of justicemaking for women and marginalized men.

No text is sacred if used to abuse, violate, or trivialize human and other earthcreatures. The christian bible is holy only insofar as we who read, study, preach, or teach it do so in a spirit of collaborative, critical inquiry steeped in collective struggle for radical mutuality between and among us all on the earth. The bible can be scripture, sacred writing, a resource for justicemaking here and now, in our own time and place. It can bear authority for christians (and others too) in relation to diverse resources (books, people, stories, memories, oral traditions, customs) that strengthen our efforts toward mutually empowering relationships.

If we study the bible with a critical eye, which we must if our minds are set on justice, we discover ways in which the eternal Wellspring of justice was or was not, is or is not, present in a particular story or interpretation.

We will know, for example, that the Spirit of justice had nothing to do with Jephthah's sacrifice of his daughter (Judges 11), the dismemberment of the concubine (Judges 19), or the offering of the daughters rather than the sons to the predatory visitors in the story of Sodom and Gomorrah (Genesis 19). Stories such as these about violence against women can be scripture only insofar as they teach us what God was and is *not* doing. We must remember that what is concealed may be as important as what is revealed in scripture.

We will know, moreover, that the sacred sensual power in our yearning for mutuality in relation to one another did not condone, much less authorize, the silencing of women in the churches (1 Corinthians), the keeping of slaves (Ephesians), or the rejection of homosexual persons (Genesis, Leviticus, Romans). What is not revealed in scripture may be as critical in our wrestling with spiritual authority as what is.

If we wish to study and present the bible as a scriptural resource in the work of justice, we should be aware that, in the hands of those who hold unjust power in place, the bible continues to be used as a bludgeon against even the impulse toward liberation from nonmutual power relations. Those whose loved ones, or whose own well-being, have been damaged by biblically approved violence, oppression, and bigotry have good reason to resist angrily any attempt to present the christian bible as a (much less *the*) liberating word of God.

Christians would do well to speak less of "the bible" and more of justice. We also would do well to listen more in relation to those who, even more than we ourselves, have been put down, cast out, or worse, by well-meaning christian folks like us.

We weave our scripture out of *phantasie,* a blend of intuition and what feminist theologian Alison Cheek has named "historical imagination."[15] This may move christians beyond claiming the bible alone as our scripture, though we may choose to include it as part of our scriptural authority, and we may allow it to participate in shaping our spiritual authority. But we may also allow other resources to meet us as word, sound, vision, and sense of the sacred Spirit. Indeed, we must, if we are interested seriously in justice for women, gaymen, and lesbians, and if we desire deeply to celebrate our erotic connectedness.

Womanist ethicist Katie Cannon told me seven years ago that Alice Walker's *The Color Purple* had become part of her sacred canon.[16] At about the same time, womanist theologian Delores Williams challenged the MudFlower Collective, which was writing *God's Fierce Whimsy,* to open our minds to the possibility of creating scripture ourselves. I heard in my sisters' words a profound wisdom that frightened me.

I am confident today that womanists like Cannon and Williams have been paving a spiritual path for all women who are committed to justice for all, and that we who are must keep our scriptures open. That means all of us who are in the struggle: of African, European, and Asian heritages; women and men; lesbians, gaymen, bisexual, and heterosexual sisters and brothers; married, celibate, single, and divorced; christian, jewish, wicca, and others. All who are committed to moving toward radical mutuality in our private and public, pastoral and political lives must be vulnerable to the possibilities of transformation. This requires that the sources and resources of our spiritual authority—our scripture—be open, with us, to change and surprise.

As a resource of spiritual authority, scripture may inform a sexual theology by inviting us to perceive the Sacred as embodied in our yearning for mutual relation. Whether it be the biblical creation stories, the book of Ruth, *The Color Purple*, or our mothers' letters to their friends, scripture reveals God's involvement in our efforts to cocreate right relation.

Gloria Naylor, in her second novel, *Linden Hills*,[17] gives us a glimpse, for instance, of a black middle-class woman who is kept in the basement of her husband's house. Isolated from all outside contact, she is moved close to the edge of madness. Her salvation emerges in her discovery of letters, bits and fragments of information, left in the basement by her husband's first wife who also had been his prisoner. No longer alone, her isolation shattered by making the connection with a sister, this woman's liberation is underway. In the spiritual company of a sister who has gone before, this woman begins to god.

Spiritual movement can be generated in our lives by, for example, a novel, film, photograph, or letter. As such our scriptural resources expand and move us along, stretching us into the realization of our radically transformative power in relation to one another. This power is our god. She is the Alpha and the Omega—the beginning and the end of wisdom, the first impulse and the last gasp in our struggles to make love, befriend, and do justice. And neither depths nor heights, nor things past nor things to come, nor principalities nor powers shall separate us from the power of this god.

We may name her Christa, as creation, suffering, and celebration of radical mutuality. Or perhaps we shall call her Sophia, Wisdom. Or we may experience him in the mystical presence of Jesus. Or in a collective womanist memory of Hagar. Or maybe we shall call it simply Justice, or by the names of other divine and holy spirits. As sacred resource, scripture opens with us and keeps us open to meeting, cocreating, and recreating new and ancient sources of learning how to love one another—how to suffer and struggle, how to celebrate and god, together.

Chapter 6

THE EROTIC AS POWER: SEXUAL THEOLOGY

The divine is always becoming flesh—what else does the Eros desire? Of course, stories of God becoming Man have eclipsed the revelation of Her becoming Woman. But now, in our becoming, vision begins slowly to clear.

—CATHERINE KELLER*

I was not raised in a religious or spiritual home. In fact, I was raised in a dysfunctional home: the family disease is alcoholism. . . . I have both the personal and family aspect of alcoholism. At age seventeen, I entered AA (Alcoholics Anonymous). . . . After seven years of sobriety, the family aspect of the disease hit bottom. . . . I learned of my childhood abuse. . . . My faith in the Higher Power was put to the test. . . . I needed faith in a new way. I began to call my Higher Power "Goddess." I started to feel and see her. I envisioned a deity who loved me. A major part of this envisioning was to see her as sexual . . . a woman who loves women and bleeds every month in sympathy with women. Part of my recovery was to realize that I was not being punished by my Higher Power. The punishment I had thought that I was living was not to be sexual in my marriage. I had thought that I had to pay the price (for what, I did not know) by not being sexual. Relationships for me had always been sexual or emotional, never both. What I began to realize was that I was a lesbian . . . twenty-five years old, beginning to be sexual for the first time in nonabusive, sensual ways. . . .

I meet God in many ways and many places. I pray. I

---

* Catherine Keller, *From a Broken Web: Separation, Sexism, and Self* (Boston: Beacon, 1986), 250.

talk throughout the day to my Higher Power. One of my
most profound experiences of Goddess is with my lover—
while we are having sex and especially during that moment
of peaking, I feel a deep sense of her presence and love
with me.

Jennifer,
theological student

I am writing between sadness and hope. My faith in you, in myself, in our sacred source seems irrepressible, though why I cannot tell in this moment, for around and within me is much despair. I'm afraid it will not be long before we know we are not exaggerating when we speak of fascism here at home. We are destroying ourselves, our flesh and blood. It is not "those people" who are shooting up with dirty needles; not "those others" taking their own lives in shame and terror; not "them" battered to within an inch of their lives. Unless we know at the core of our integrity that we are they, neither this book nor any resource on love will make much sense to us now.

Our movements through the impasses can change the world. That is why principalities and powers will move heaven and earth to secure until the end of time our fears of one another and of ourselves in right relation.

But we do not have so long to heal our broken bonds and wounded lives.

We will not find much help in our healing from the church, or from the God of christians, jews, and other patriarchal religions. The problem with this deity is that he evokes our shame and fear and then constructs rigid boundaries around us as a means of containing our feelings and our lives.

Men create this god to make themselves self-possessed; to give themselves control over chaotic forces of passion, sex, and death. And since men, like women, are in relation, their self-possession involves controlling others. This is why practitioners of patriarchal religion tend to assume control, by fear or force, of the world itself, including our bodyselves, psyches, and souls: the places in us in which our lives are transformed if we can reach through the fear to one another.

Although recent studies suggest that certain movements in the early church may not have been wholly erotophobic, the relation between God and the erotic, spirituality and sexuality, in the history of christian control is largely one of violent opposition.[1] As a chaotic and passionate resource, sex must be controlled by whatever means necessary: such has been a dominant christian motif. Christians have learned and inwardly digested the repressive lesson that God is good and sex is bad. Irrespective of our religious traditions, we westerners have been christianized, all of us, and have absorbed through our bodies sexual taboos such as those set forth by the Council of Elvira (381 C.E.). See chapter 3 on the Council of Elvira.

Questions about the opposition between the christian God and sex lead to Augustine (354–430 C.E.). While Elvira was the first ecclesial body to legislate explicitly against sexuality, Augustine, Bishop of Hippo, was the first theologian to systematize erotophobia—fear of sex—as a staple (arguably *the* staple) of christian orthodoxy.[2]

Augustine was a brilliant, faithful North African who, being "born again" as a young man, renounced sexual activity and the dualistic Manichean religion and moved into a celibate life and the christian faith he was learning from such teachers as Ambrose.[3]

Augustine was split in his own conversion and consequently left a disintegrated legacy of sexual versus spiritual passion: He seems to have been a man of sexual passion. He had a mistress whom he loved, and he had a son with her. We know he had strong spiritual passion. Upon conversion, he took both passions obsessively with him: his spirituality as a source of love and creativity; his sexuality as a source of shame and guilt.

Augustine had turned spiritually away from the Manichean belief that good and evil are locked in eternal combat. But, far from renouncing the implications of this dualistic cosmology, he had turned to embrace a dualistic (spiritual versus sexual) morality, which he experienced as essential to his new-found belief in one (spiritual, good) God.

For the convert Augustine, the cosmos was no longer dualistic (God alone is both good and powerful); but the realm of human affairs was as split as ever—perhaps more so, for we now had only ourselves (no cosmic evil power) to blame for the lust, pride, and other vainglories of human being. As prisoners of our wills, we had become *non posse non peccare* (not able not to sin). We had become, in fact, a *massa damnata*—a damned mass. If there were any single, most reprehensible, cause of our corruption as a species, it had been our *concupiscence*, our experience of sexuality.

Augustine was confused, spiritually and sexually. This we can assert fairly from a feminist perspective. His *spiritual* confusion was, as he knew, a consequence of his failure to take seriously the vast, just, merciful, and mysterious character of the Sacred. What Augustine did not know was that his *sexual* confusion, which increasingly he denied and which, therefore, took up increasingly more space in his life, work, and legacy, was rooted in the same failure to apprehend the same character of the same God.

Rather than embracing sexuality as a dimension of sacred passion, Augustine targeted it as its opposite: the source of sin, setting in theological motion a violent antagonism, which christians (and others) have suffered to this day. Split in his passion, disintegrated at the root, the converted Augustine (followed by christian men for 1,600 years) made the connections wrong—between sex and God.[4] This chapter is a small effort to help make them right.[5]

Theology, the study of God, is about making connections—sensual and erotic as well as conceptual.[6] I've attempted thus far to make connections between social, historical, and theological apprehensions, and distortions, of erotic power. In this chapter, I explore the character of the erotic as sacred power, or the sense in which God is erotic power.

In traditional systematic theological discourse, doctrines of creation and redemption/liberation are distinct, though related, doctrines. In my work, while "creation/creative" and "liberation/liberating" bear different nuances, which derive from their more conventional usages, they do not refer to separate moments or events in either human or divine life. They signal sacred process. They signal relational empowerment, which is at once creative and liberating, sensual and sacred.

This process is creative because it brings us into embodied realization of ourselves in relation: It creates us. As transcendent relational movement, this erotic process liberates us from our daily senses of being stuck in, and deadened by, alienated social relations and theological mindsets such as those discussed in chapters 2, 3, and 4.

Living creative/liberating lives as individuals does not eliminate, of course, the problem of alienation. From a traditional christian perspective, this is the problem of original sin—the vast, global character of the structures of domination and subjugation that permeate the foundations of our life together. But our personal relational efforts toward liberation can empower us to resist the evil generated by our lack of mutuality, our sin, and can contribute to the cultivation of a sacred realm of right relation that is both here and not here yet.

This affirmation and lament—the "yet/not yet" of our mutuality—might be read traditionally as a doctrine of "last things," or eschatology. It reflects the moral and temporal ambiguities of our lives, as well as faith in our movement toward what is not yet realized among us. Our relational vision remains unfulfilled. The erotic continues to be distorted, wreaking abuse and confusion among us. We do not yet live perfectly in the realm of the sacred and, in this world, we never will. Yet we are drawn toward the possibility of living more fully together as friends and lovers. We believe that this possibility is within our reach, and our faith is not merely idle speculation. We are not deluded. We move toward that which, through intimations and glimpses, intuitions and relationships, we know *already* to be real.

Yet sometimes, it is true, it seems as if we do not live even partially in the sacred realm of right relation, so stuck are we in the fear of mutuality and its consequence, sadomasochistic relations, which characterize not only the "might makes right" credo of our national government but also, not infrequently, our own most intimate friendships. To live through these dynamics of alienated power toward the realization of our power in right relation is not merely to focus, however, on "last things." We do not move toward a final, static, resolution of our relational fears and tensions. To the contrary, our power draws us into our beginnings—into the heart of our creation/creativity, into our relatedness.[7] Here we participate in liberating one another from the isolation, brokenness, and despair wrought by abusive power relations in the great and small places of our lives.

In the last part of this chapter, the image of Christa—creative/liberating, passionate woman—will be presented as a transitional christian symbol of sacred power.[8] Christa may help christians envision more clearly our power in mutual relation as *christic* power— the radically mutual power by which, through which, and with which we participate in creating and blessing, healing and liberating, one another.

Broken and deformed by abuse and fear, we are Christa: called/calling forth by the wild, compelling vision, or perhaps only the dim memory or faint hope, of one another's real presence in history, in time/space, in our lives as persons in relation. By the grace of this christic power in relation, we risk participating in our own creation/liberation. In so doing, battered and bruised though we are, we may form with one another, from a christian perspective, the soulful, sensual body of Christa—which is a sacred/christic movement of *compañeras*, a holy communion of friends, a spirited resource of hope for the earth and for its many, varied creatures.

Daring to risk sharing this life together, coming into our YES, anointing one another's wounds as healers, each in her own way, we discover with greater confidence the authority among us that can be trusted to help us sustain our power in mutual relation. Steeped in the sacred relational spirit that has moved and empowered friends and lovers from the beginning, we yearn to be true to ourselves in relation, touched by and touching one another in the soul of who we are together and in each of our deepest places.[9]

Walking with my dogs, I become aware in a fresh way of how marvelous it is to be a member of a "group"—women—which, along with blacks and animals, has been associated closely in western history with "nature." Not that wind and water and fire and earth are simply or always benign, because they are not. Nature can be cruel and deadly—human nature especially. And each of us dies in our own embodied way, which is seldom easy. But keeping slow pace with my older dog, Teraph, I know what I have in common with the trees' gnarled roots at the water's edge, the wind-chill whipping my cheeks, the pile of dog shit I step in, the crows harping from the fence, the joggers and other walkers, some smiling and nodding, others preoccupied and aloof. I know them all, the people and the trees. I do not know their names, but I know that our sensuality, our shared embodied participation in forming and sustaining the relational matrix that is our home on this planet, is our most common link, and that our sensuality can be trusted.

If we learn to trust our senses, our capacities to touch, taste, smell, hear, see, and thereby know, they can teach us what is good and what is bad, what is real and what is false, for us in relation to one another and to the earth and cosmos. I say to myself, as I return to campus from my outing with my dogs, that sensuality is a foundation for our authority.

Our power in relation reveals herself through our senses and feelings, the basic resources of our intelligence, a relational quality with origins in our capacities to live responsibly in relation to one another. The quality of our intelligence is embedded in feeling connected to one another. Our feelings are evoked and strengthened sensually by touching, tasting, hearing, seeing, and smelling *with* one another. Our senses and the feelings that are generated by them become primary spiritual resources. In knowing one another through our senses, feelings, and intelligence—and intuition is a form of intelligence—we come to know God.[10]

God reveals herself through our relationships not only to other people but also to other creatures and nature. This is a faith-claim that is both in continuity and discontinuity with those of traditional western christianity. Its continuity is in the emphasis on revelation through incarnation; its discontinuity is in stressing the sacred character of nature—flesh, dirt, wetness, sex, woman.[11] The erotic is known most immediately through our senses. We see, hear, touch, smell, and taste the divine, who is embodied between and among us insofar as we are moving more fully into, or toward, mutually empowering relationships in which all creatures are accorded profound respect and dignity.

The erotic fabric of our lives in relation has not been treated affirmatively in the history of christian life and thought. The incarnation is not taken seriously, even in Jesus' life, much less as the basic character structure of all creation. The incarnation of God in Jesus has been interpreted historically as an essentially spiritual act, in which Jesus' bodyself ("flesh") got spiritualized.[12] The god whom christians believe to be the source of love and justice in the universe did not materialize for long, if at all, in Jesus. "Christ" became historically the symbol by which we know that Jesus' spiritualization was accomplished as a unique and singular event: Only Jesus is Christ; he and he alone is Lord of the Universe, according to christian teachings.

The christian bible was canonized, and is used still, to support this process of spiritualization. A major problem, therefore, with using the bible as a primary resource for authority among justice-seeking christians is that it is weighted, especially in the New Testament, toward the spiritualization—trivialization and denial—of our bodyselves. The effect of this process is damaging to all people whose self-images are shaped in cultures dominated by christianity, which is all of us in the United States.

To deny the sacred power of our embodied yearnings is to be pulled away from one another and hence from ourselves. To have our bodyselves trivialized and demeaned is to be snatched out of our senses and alienated from our erotic desires. This process of alienation from our sacred power produces antierotic (or pornographic) psyches and lives, in which our bodies and feelings are jerked off by abusive power dynamics: domination, coercion, and violence.

Where then do we turn for help in healing our broken bonds and wounded lives? To whom do we look for images of sacred power, mutuality, and friendship? We come to our senses, quite literally, and we look to our people and other creatures as well. But who are they, these friends to whom we are accountable in our theologies and ethics and in living our daily lives?

To hold oneself accountable is to make a moral claim on the basis of our values (what we believe to be good); our obligations (the constraints that respect for one another set on our actions); and our vision (our images of life as we seek to create/liberate our life together on the basis of our values and obligations). It is on the basis of these foundations that we are drawn, consciously or not, toward certain people, processes, and resources, and not toward others, in framing the authority for our theological and ethical claims.

These three basic dimensions of our moral lives—forged out of our lives in relation to past, present, and future generations of people, other creatures, and our cocreative power—are the primary resource for our spiritual and theological authority. Never simply our own private opinions, our values, obligations, and visions are created and recreated constantly in our relational matrix, in which—along with our values, obligations, and visions—we are growing in relation to those whose lives we trust. We see them, hear them, learn from them, teach them, and know ourselves as connected to them in value-enhancing ways.

I am accountable to those who are committed to justice *for all.* This does not mean that I live this value very evenly or very well. Most of us do not. But the commitment is honest and strong. The promise that draws me to such people is that they will remind me of the limits of what I can know and of the fact that, even when I believe I'm being inclusive in my work, someone is being left out. To the extent that this "someone" has been left out historically, repeatedly and as a matter of course, I am helping hold unjust power in place even in my honest outpourings for justice.

I see the value of justice—right, mutual, relation—borne out in the lives of those with whom I choose to stand, those whose lives bear concrete specific witness: for example, in the efforts of anti-racist workers; in the commitment of those who resist the contras; in the vitality and justice-centered issues of Jesse Jackson's 1988 campaign; in the struggles of battered women who have had enough; in liberation work in South Africa, Korea, the Soviet Union, El Salvador, Iran, the United States, Israel; in the movement of lesbians and gaymen who are coming out.

I see mutuality/justice embodied by an old man who cares for his dogs and is grateful for what they give him. I recognize mutuality in a heterosexual friend's refusal to say she is not a lesbian when asked by her bishop. I hear mutuality in music celebrating the whales and the earth. I am moved by the mutuality in the commitment of some christian feminists to expunge anti-Semitism from their worship and their lives.

I see mutuality borne out in the lives of women and men raising their children to befriend rather than fear the world, its human and other creatures, and at the same time to take care of themselves and one another in a world often hostile to gentle people. I know mutuality is lived out as one friend sits with another dying of AIDS; I watch this same commitment flash in the eyes of a woman working the streets of Spanish Harlem, giving bleach to addicts for their needles, to help protect them from the deadly HIV virus.

I experience mutuality with my students who are coming together with one another and me into new questions and clarifications of a shared vocation as teachers and preachers of good news to marginalized and oppressed persons and to those in solidarity with them. I know mutuality with my own teachers and healers who with me continue to come into our power to learn and mend together so that we can make a difference in a world that needs our friendship as testimony to a relational power that is trustworthy.

I stand with those whose politics and spirituality I have come to trust: those who know that we meet the Sacred in relation to one another, and who understand that any power that we or others use in ways that are not mutually empowering is abusive. I look to such women and men, of whatever color, religion, class, sexual preference or orientation, to confirm in me a joyful commitment to live responsibly in this world.

With these people, I envision a world/church in which the lamb and lion will be friends, a time/space in which healing and forgiveness, touching and pleasure, celebration and justice, will be far more universally available than any of these relational blessings are among us today.

These are people to whom I am accountable in discerning resources for authority in my life—for helping me separate out the wheat from the chaff, the true from the false. My people have led me to Elie Wiesel's *Night*, Adrienne Rich's *On Lies, Secrets and Silence*, Julia Esquivel's *Threatened with Resurrection*, Gloria Naylor's *Women of Brewster Place*, Audre Lorde's *Sister Outsider*, Dorothee Sölle's *Beyond Mere Obedience*, and Beverly Harrison's *Making the Connections*.[13] Such books have become staples in my canon of scripture and their authors have become my people.

My people have shown me that racism is more than wrong, it is evil—and so is what our nation is doing to the poor of the world in Guatemala, Angola, Korea, and in these United States. They suggest to me that class injury cuts to the core of our life together and leaves us wounded and hurt in ways invisible to the vast majority of United States citizens, *especially* those of us with ready access to economic survival resources.[14]

My people remind me of my roots, my limits, my gifts, and my questions. They help keep me humble—connected, that is, to others, and aware that we are a commonpeople. My people pull me toward the margins of the church, academia, and the disciplines, to the margins even of movements for justice.

My people keep me growing and expect me to be relationally aware. They ask me to be honest with them about what I am doing, what I yearn for, what my commitments are, what I delight in, what I am willing to suffer for, if need be die for—and what I am trying, therefore, to live for. My people ask me to realize and celebrate ways in which my accountability is reliable, trustworthy, and empowering to them as well as to me, which it is not consistently or always.

My people embody, for me, the real presence of sacred movement, enabling me to stand and bend not merely with the oppressed but with all who are struggling against unjust power relations. With my people—friends, *compañeras*, sisters and brothers, known and unknown—I realize that our creative power in relation, the power of our godding, is the wellspring of our sexualities: our yearnings to embody mutually empowering relations, our desire to live into our YES.

Christian theology traditionally has held that *eros* (sexual love) and *philia* ("brotherly" love, or friendship) are *at best* forms of love derivative from, and less godly, than *agape* (God's love for us, and ours for God and neighbor—"neighbor" being interpreted frequently as those who are hard to love: "humankind" in general, "the poor," our "enemies").[15] The moral distinction among the three forms of love is fastened in classical christian dualisms between spiritual and material/physical reality, between self and other. There is, moreover, a concomitant assumption that it is more difficult—therefore better—to express God's spiritual love of enemies, strangers, and people we may not enjoy than to love our friends and sexual partners.

In these pages, I am not attempting simply to rearrange the traditional christian categories of love. I am suggesting that these distinctions represent a radical misapprehension of love, which is at once divine and human. The traditional christian understanding of love fails to value adequately the embodied human experience of love among friends and sexual partners *because* it assumes the negative, dangerous, and nonspiritual character of sensual, erotic, and sexual feelings and expressions.

The erotic is our most fully embodied experience of the love of God. As such, it is the source of our capacity for transcendence, the "crossing over" among ourselves, making connections between ourselves in relation.[16] The erotic is the divine Spirit's yearning, through our bodyselves, toward mutually empowering relation, which is our most fully embodied experience of God as love (First Letter of John, 4:7 ff). Regardless of who may be the lovers, the root of the love is sacred movement between and among us. This love is agapic, philial, and erotic. It is God's love and, insofar as we embody and express it, it is ours.[17]

Love may or may not be embodied among those who give bread to the poor. Love may or may not be incarnate between people in the excited throes of genital sex. Insofar as our relationships are not steeped in a longing to share in such a way that each person is enabled to be herself, the Sacred is muted and diminished among us. Mutuality is our shared experience of power in relation. By it we are called forth more fully into becoming who we are—whole persons with integrity, together. Our shared power is sacred power, and it is erotic.

Our shared experience of relational power, our sacred experience of sensual power, our erotic experience of the power of God, is the root of our theological epistemology. It is the basis of our knowledge and love of God. It is a calling forth, an occasion to touch each other's lives, and an open invitation into the healing of common woundedness:

So let us light a red candle between us. Let us sit patiently together at a distance. Let us imagine the possibility, the value, the goodness, and the joy in our healing. Let us envision ourselves moving through fear to participate in creating and liberating, blessing and transforming, one another and the world around us—in small ways, and perhaps in ways not so small.

Let us wait with one another on the Spirit.

I know this relational way is not easy. The christian fathers were right about this, but for the wrong reason. With Augustine, they have believed that loving is hard because, in order to love, we must renounce or at least control our erotic passion.

In fact, loving is hard because learning to share our passion, the exuberant yearnings of our erotic/sacred power, requires of us, in Dorothee Sölle's words, "revolutionary patience" *with* one another, not renunciation of ourselves or others.[18] It takes a great deal of time and love for us to learn how to let go of our senses of separateness, isolation, and self-control, and risk not only reaching out to touch others but also allowing ourselves to be touched deeply by them.

We need revolutionary patience, with ourselves and with one another, if we are to help each other learn to respect and cross the boundaries of our bodyselves, the qualities of personal integrity that render each of us unique and, in this sense, separate from all others. We are not the same, not in the beginning, not in the end. We are not one, not a merger, not a unity of look-alike-think-alike-act-alike-be-alike.

In the beginning is the relation, not sameness.

In the beginning is tension and turbulence, not easy peace.

In the beginning, our erotic power moves us to touch, not take over; transform, not subsume. We are empowered by a longing not to blur the contours of our differences, but rather to reach through the particularities of who we are toward our common strength, our shared vulnerability, and our relational pleasure.

Calling us forth, the Holy One blesses us with one another's presence and, through the relation, with sharper senses of ourselves as individuals.[19]

Learning these relational lessons *with* one another is the only way we can learn them. It is the only way we can experience the love of God, the creative energy of our godding, the erotic as sacred power.

Audre Lorde speaks of erotic power as "an assertion of the life-force of women; of that creative energy empowered, the knowledge and use of which we are now reclaiming in one language, our history, our dancing, our loving, our work, our lives." She associates the erotic with wisdom, "the nurturer or nursemaid of all our deepest knowledge" and, again, with creativity: "There is, for me, no difference between writing a good poem and moving into sunlight against the body of a woman I love."[20]

Though it is neither her purpose nor her desire to speak of "God," Lorde writes brilliantly of (and, I am sure, with passionate desire for) the Sacred. This woman knows the erotic as sacred power: life-force, creative energy, nursemaid of wisdom.

She notes the traditional (christian, though she does not name it so) split between the spiritual and the erotic, by which we have

reduc[ed] the spiritual to a world of flattened affect, a world of the ascetic who aspires to feel nothing. But nothing is farther from the truth. For the ascetic position is one of the highest fear, the gravest immobility. The severe abstinence of the ascetic becomes the ruling obsession. And it is one not of self-discipline but of self-abnegation.[21]

Recognizing the fear-laden conditions of our lives in a culture of alienation and isolation, Lorde warns,

We have been raised to fear the *yes* within ourselves, our deepest cravings. . . . The fear of our desires keeps them suspect and indiscriminately powerful, for to suppress any truth is to give it strength beyond endurance. The fear that we cannot grow beyond whatever distortions we may find within ourselves keeps us docile and loyal and obedient, externally defined, and leads us to accept many facets of our oppression as women.[22]

She recognizes and names our problems, the dynamics that divide us and fasten us unaware in antagonistic opposition between sexuality and spirituality: Christians and nearly everyone else in christianized culture have been taught "to fear the YES within ourselves"; to fear and deny "our deepest cravings" and strongest feelings; to embody an obsession against these feelings and desires; to abnegate ourselves, blotting out who we are in favor of a "docility, loyalty, and obedience" to external authorities and to the "distortions within ourselves" that have been shaped by these authorities.

Even our inner voices, which we may call "conscience" or "God," "ethics" or "intuition," are trained to speak in the spirit of homage to a fear that is invisible to us. It is our fear of our YES to our own life force. We fear this life force, our erotic power, because, if celebrated rather than denied, our YES would "force us to evaluate [all aspects of our existence] honestly in terms of their relative meaning within our lives."[23]

Our lives would be transformed. Nothing would remain the same. For, as Lorde affirms, "Once we begin to feel deeply all the aspects of our lives, we begin to demand from ourselves and from our life-pursuits that they feel in accordance with that joy which we know ourselves to be capable of."[24] The capacity to begin moving through fear toward our YES is a blessing. It is the beginning of healing, the dawning of new creation.

As we come to experience the erotic as sacred, we begin to know ourselves as holy and to imagine ourselves sharing in the creation of one another and of our common well-being. As we recognize the faces of the Holy in the faces of our lovers and friends, as well as in our own, we begin to feel at ease in our bodyselves—sensual, connected, and empowered. We become resources with one another of a wisdom and a pleasure in which heretofore we have not dared believe.

We begin to realize that God moves among us, transcending our particularities. She is born and embodied in our midst. She is ground and figure, power and person, this creative Spirit, root of our commonlife and of our most intensely personal longings.[25] As the wind blows across the ocean, stirring up the seacreatures, causing them to tumble, rearranging them, the erotic crosses over among us, moving us to change the ways we are living in relation. Touched by this sacred power, we are never the same again.

Yes, our erotic power is sacred power because it is transcendent. She connects us in our most profoundly human, most deeply embodied, soulful places, making us who we are: a relational body of incarnate love.

Through the real, daily presence and yearnings of our bodyselves, this sacred power is involved intimately in the lives of both women and men. God is not, therefore, above sex or gender, but rather is immersed in our gendered and erotic particularities. Therefore it is appropriate and can be helpful to personalize divinity by ascribing to her or him a fluid sense of gender, an image than can change on the basis of human need.[26] I refer to God in these pages as "she" partly to compensate in tiniest measure for the overwhelming extent to which the deity remains "he" in christian tradition.

And there is another, closely related, historically compelling reason in this book for envisioning the Spirit as creative womanpower: Because woman has been associated *negatively* in western history and religion with embodied feeling and sexuality, the power of this historically pejorative association can be transformed and sustained—*for good purpose*—by women. This can happen by the creative/liberating power that is incarnate in mutual relation. Through the moral witness borne intrinsically in erotic friendship, the association of womanpower with strong, embodied feeling can be, and is already, experienced as a resource of profound spiritual transformation.

Linking ourselves as women with body and nature and darkness and moisture and dirt and sex can illuminate the Sacred: She can be for us, in this predominantly white western male historical moment, a resource of womanpower that is passionate, dark, and intelligent; sensual, juicy, and big; wise, good-humored, and outraged at abusive power relations. Through her relational longings, we may be drawn into our own.

To experience or envision God as an empowered/empowering female presence constitutes a transcendent leap from a fear of strong, women-affirming women to a profound appreciation of women who manifest women-inspired, women-loving, relational energy in our love and work. Perhaps the erotic power of God will be most often the dark, woman-loving-women energy among us as long as we are living under heterosexist, racist patriarchy. If so, it will be this way for a long time.

Let us enjoy her and delight in her erotic love! Let us embody her power and learn, with her, to make no peace with oppression. Among christians, she may be Christa, or we may know her by other names.

But most of us are so frightened of harm, of being badly hurt, and of hurting others. And so we resist the sacred eros.

O, my sister, what madness tears at the heart of God! at my heart and yours!

We are together in this fear, you and I. We are its captives— and we, its liberators.

So come. Let us wait for God together.

This sense of sacred purpose is not simply mine, or ours. It is the aim of God herself: to create the friendship in which the cosmos is originally imaged. I mean by "original" not simply first, but purposive: We are created originally for (the purpose of) friendship.[27]

To generate friendship—embodied/incarnate mutuality—is the purpose of a sexual theology and ethics, just as it is the heart of a liberating God. We need to understand more about what mutuality is, and what it is not, to realize what is involved in our liberation.[28]

As Margaret Huff and others have noted, mutuality is not merely reciprocity, a *quid pro quo* give and take of benefits or sexual pleasure.[29] Nor is mutuality a way of being in relation without anger or conflict. It is a process of relational movement that most often is charged with tension. It is a process in which two or more people are struggling to share power between/among ourselves.

Mutuality involves wrestling more fully to embody friendship. It involves learning to stand and walk together and to recognize and honor the differences we bring to our commonground. It requires risking *through* fear, not without it, to be friends. It means working together on our frustrations, hurt, anger, confusion, and conflicts.

Mutuality is a process of getting unstuck, of moving through impasses, of coming into our power together. It is the way of liberation, of calling forth the best in one another and, in so doing, of empowering one another to be who we are at our best.

Mutuality is the process by which we create and liberate one another. It is not only about lesbian or gay relationships. (Some of us have tended to idealize the mutuality in lesbian bonding.)[30] It is about heterosexual relating, it is about black-white, Hispanic-Anglo, and Asian-European relating.

The erotic is not only movement toward mutuality. It involves a yearning or longing for mutuality.[31] "Yearning" implies a desire for something we don't yet have, don't quite know how to participate in, or don't experience fully as ours. The term "longing" may further sharpen the eschatological movement of the erotic, in which we long for something that, in mutual relation, is both yet—and not yet, both now—and coming. Such relationships may be charged with tensions steeped in unequal power dynamics. Mutuality often involves working out inequality—in work, in love, in sex.

Sadomasochism is a social structure of alienated power.[32] In it people learn to accept, as natural and even as enjoyable, possessing (sadistic) power-over or (masochistic) power-under others.[33] To exploit or be exploited in this way is to be in wrong relation.

We live in a praxis of alienation, or wrong relation, from which we cannot escape. All of us are, to some significant degree, in bondage to wrong relation, alienated power relations, which frequently we do not recognize as problematic. Those who are justice-minded tend to perceive the alienation in racism, sexism, and other transparently oppressive structures of alienated power. But we have more trouble realizing ways in which these structures have shaped our own psyches and spiritualities, our capacities for friendship and sexual pleasure.

Right relation, or mutuality, is not a static way of being in op-position to wrong relation. Mutuality is a relational process of mov-ing through sadomasochism, in which the energy for domination/submission is transformed erotically into power for sharing. Mu-tuality is a way of redirecting wrong relational power.

Sadomasochistic sensibilities need not be denied. They are the raw material out of which are formed relationships in which people, slowly and partially, are able to experience—share and feel—love without pain. In this sense, mutually empowering relationships may well embody sadomasochistic dynamics. In attempting to express deep relational yearning beyond the pain inherent to domination/submission toward the peace of feeling safe, caring, and cared for, men and women often must struggle fiercely with friends and lovers and with themselves.

We cannot simply lift our embodied feelings out of a world that has alienated us, broken us, and *at best* given us conflicting feelings about ourselves and others, our own worth, and that of others. We cannot make ourselves feel what we do not. We cannot make our-selves "feel mutual" in perfect, constant, or unambivalent ways in a social order fastened in alienated power. Our bodyselves know better. They speak the truth.

We often feel humiliated, beaten, and diminished, because we are members of an abusive society. All of us have been abused by somebody or something at sometime, most frequently within the dominant institutions of our lives (religious, educational, medical, legal, martial, marital). Our eroticism is affected by our experiences of power in relation to these institutions and people.

As suggested in chapter 3, people who attempt to live deeply into their power in relation characteristically learn to associate this effort toward mutual empowerment with pain. This is because, in a praxis of alienation and domination, the desire for mutuality almost in-variably is punished rather than rewarded.

We do not learn mutuality as our natural way of being. To the extent that, through faith and experience, we come to believe in the sacred power of relationships in which we nurture one another's growth, we are planting seeds. As we learn to harvest their fruit together, we will transform the social order. This revolutionary possibility frightens honest people, because it requires that their most personal, daily relationships be transformed.

Revolutionary relationships require that we be real with one another, really present with one another, and honest. It is in our unacknowledged fear of radical personal change that we often hurt those who, by being real with us, are inviting us to be the same. Sometimes this is a role that children play in our lives. Calling us forth into our least hidden, most spontaneous selves, they invite us to be ourselves with them. In relation to children or to our adult peers, we may be terrified of what we desire most heartily—to love and be loved for who we really are. Acting out of this sad fear, we may punish the very ones who offer us this opportunity.

And so, in our life together in this society, we learn masochism. Associating efforts to be ourselves, attempts to be real, with punishment and pain, we learn an embodied emotional connection between the erotic yearning to become more deeply rooted in relational power and the meting out of punishment: whippings, deprivation, humiliation, rejection.

We also learn sadism. We learn not only to fear the friendship and intimacy that may call us more fully into ourselves, but also to deny that we are afraid. To this extent, we are excellent students of sadism, unable not to abuse those in our lives who offer us opportunities to be ourselves with them. We learn to enjoy the "power" in separating and distancing ourselves from those who display their own, and represent our, vulnerability: children, women, differently abled men and women, gaymen and lesbians, animals, students, patients, prisoners, poor people, elderly people, members of racial, ethnic, cultural, or religious minorities.

As a psychopathology, sadomasochism has been associated with individuals—sadism with "perverse men"; masochism with women. Surely most women and many men in heterosexist patriarchy are educated by life, as well as by school and religion, to be masochistic. But while our sadomasochism is pathological, the disease is not primarily one of individuals. Sadomasochism belongs to the whole society. It is our pathology, our problem. Only with each other's help and good humor can we begin to struggle through the enormity of the pain most people have learned to associate with love.

But can sadomasochistic eroticism be a relational conduit through which we move toward mutuality not only with each other but also with God, the source of our liberation? The answer is that it *must* be, because we can reach one another and God only from where we are here and now. Only from this present place, broken and battered as we may be, can we reach toward one another and ourselves and be really in touch with the knowledge and love of God, our power in right relation.

"Having sex," if it is erotic, is about power-sharing. As such, it involves journeying together through places of brokenness and pain toward safety and tenderness. Sadomasochistic eroticism does not signal necessarily that something is wrong with us individually, but rather indicates, unmistakably, how fundamentally formed we are—emotionally, spiritually, physically—by the world we inhabit. We cannot journey entirely beyond sadomasochism because the culture breeds it faster than we are able to imagine expunging it from our midst, either as a people or as individuals.

Most people in the United States do not realize that much of their "personal" pain has roots in the massive, systemic character of alienated power reflected, for example, in Ronald Reagan's hell-bent determination that a small, poor nation like Nicaragua "cry uncle." We are inclined rather to individualize and privatize pain as our own business and, as such, to tuck our sexual fantasies away in closets of lonely shame.

My concern is not basically with *sexual* sadomasochistic (s/m) cultures among heterosexual people, gaymen, or lesbians, but rather with the broader sense in which sadomasochism has de-formed us all as a people. There seems to me no question, however, that the larger social context of sadomasochism has helped create the sexual s/m cultures, infusing many women and men with an embodied confusion of violence and ecstasy. This is, at the very least, a *dangerous* confusion—emotionally and sometimes physically.

Whether sexual s/m is also a *moral* confusion—that is, whether it is always wrong—seems to me a complicated question with no easy or fixed answer. It is wrong physically or emotionally to hurt one another purposely, knowingly to abuse one another's bodies or psyches, whether or not "with mutual consent." But is it wrong to explore together the limits of our capacities for pleasure, or pain? To struggle together in the tensions and pathos of being more or less in control of our lives, dreams, and destinies? Such explorations can take the shape of s/m fantasies and activities. They do not seem to me necessarily wrong, just very deeply human in an honest, poignant, even at times playful way.[34]

But how can we play so vulnerably together in the midst of such fully human pathos? How can we be together in these struggles, dreams, pains, and pleasures, at once so complicated and so primitive, without abusing one another? Or can we? These are profound moral questions not simply about sex, or about s/m, but about our life together as friends and comrades on this planet.

We need to be tender with one another, and radically empathetic, especially in relation to our erotic yearnings, fears, and conflicts. We should not accuse or judge ourselves or one another of being "wrong" or "bad" in our sadomasochistic fantasies or activities with consenting adults.[35]

We yearn for mutuality. We have seen it through a glass dimly. We know it is here among us, and not here; now, but not yet. We live in these tensions of affirmation and lamentation. What we want most terrifies us most—passionate connectedness with one another that will draw us sharply into our identities as persons in relation in our work and in our love. Our way to god, through the moral clutter of alienation, is *with* one another's solidarity, in faith that none of us is alone. As our sacred power, the erotic pulls us toward this embodied realization.

What then of our differences and separate places, our boundaries, the lines between us that render each of us distinct? What does it mean to focus (as many feminist therapists do) on boundaries in the context of a social and economic order that seals us apart not merely by boundaries, but by walls that divide us? What do boundaries mean in the context of sexual and physical abuse against women and children?[36]

Sexual relationships are often abusive. This is the case whenever the bodily integrity of any person—woman, child, or, less fre- · quently in heterosexist patriarchy, adult man—is violated.[37] Movement toward mutuality is especially difficult when we lack a sense of our bodily integrity, confidence that our bodies are ours, and that we can choose with whom to share our bodyselves via touch, taste, other senses, and strong feelings.

A sense of boundaries can enable us to be confident of our bodily integrity. It can enhance our ability to participate in mutually empowering relationships. Boundaries can help us know ourselves in relation, what we enjoy and what we don't, what we want and what we don't. Only insofar as I experience my feelings of pleasure *as mine* (not, for example, as simply a reflection of yours), can I enjoy the power of the erotic as she crosses over from my body to yours, and yours to mine, blessing us both in the sensual integrity of who each of us is, as well as of who we are together.

Without a boundaried sense of ourselves, we are likely to experience sexual energy as a rush into which we simply get sucked and swallowed up, or as an addictive commodity that we have to get more of in order to feel good about ourselves. In the first instance, we lose touch with ourselves. Historically, this has happened to most women. Sexism itself is a structure of sexual abuse, in which women's lives get swept away in currents of male domination, male visibility, male possession, male naming, and male definitions of power, women, sex, and God. In the second case, we grab "sex" wherever we can get it and wind up with little or nothing that enables us to enjoy or respect ourselves very much. Erotic power can't be grabbed.

To violate sexually the boundaries of another person is evil: the absence of mutual relation.[38] Sexual violation comes in many forms and is most often perpetrated by men against women and children whom they know, frequently their own wives and children.

As a term denoting sexual permission, "mutual consent" presupposes a quality not merely of willingness, but also of desire, together with a capacity (emotional, physical, political) to say no as well as yes to the possibility of sex. A child is incapable of "mutual consent" in relation to an adult's sexual agenda.[39]

When women, children, and victimized men (gaymen, mentally handicapped men, men of color, prisoners) have their boundaries violated, they are often left with little sense of bodily integrity. As a result, they may not experience themselves as capable of mutual relation when opportunities for mutuality arise. To compound the problem, survivors of sexual abuse often are treated professionally as if the violation of their boundaries has rendered them perpetual victims, who forever must be treated more carefully than other people. There is no question that abuse survivors need strong support and care from friends, lovers, and professional helpers; but the last thing they need is to be perceived and treated as if they cannot move beyond the posture of victimization toward becoming genuinely mutual friends, partners, colleagues, persons in right relation to others, including their helpers.

If survivors cling to the perception of themselves as victims, they will be exactly that: postured eternally as powerless women or men, rather than as feisty survivors committed to seeking and finding mutuality, intimacy, and justice for themselves and others.

All women in heterosexist patriarchy are abused in one form or another. Those molested or raped by violent, troubled people have experienced particularly vicious manifestations of a universal problem that diminishes the capacities of *all* women to love and work with a sense of confidence that we are safe.

Once we are aware of the importance of boundaries in relation to our bodily integrity and safety, we need to avoid an uncritical use of the concept of "boundaries" as invariably good for our mental health.[40] There would seem to be a parallel between the current therapeutic emphasis on boundaries and boundary violation and the heralding of separation, self, and autonomy as worthy aims for women seeking personal growth and healing. There is, as Janet Surrey notes, danger in trying to protect ourselves by reinforcing the illusory legacy of white privileged western males that any of us can, or should, be a self, separated sharply from others.[41] It is good to protect ourselves from harm, but we should not live as prisoners of fear. It is also good—and far less common among white people in the United States—to do what we can toward creating a safer relational environment, in which we can live together. Feminist psychologist Susan DeMattos suggests wisely that our safety is secured by the quality of our connectedness, not by the tenacity of our separateness.[42]

Margaret Huff has remarked that boundaries can serve either as walls or as connections between us.[43] Boundaries are important, but we cannot create them unilaterally if they are to help us experience strong, empowering connectedness. To sustain mutuality, we must create our boundaries *with* one another. This is true whether we are individuals or nations. We learn, with one another's support, how to respect boundaries. We learn, with one another, how to cross them and how to expand them, how to strengthen them and how to loosen them. In Great Britain, "no trespassing" signs do not mean "keep out," as they do in the United States. Rather, they mean simply, "You are welcome to enter, but do no harm."[44] Crossing boundaries is not assumed to be synonymous with danger or harm. In fact, to refuse to cross them, to wall ourselves off from honest connectedness, can, and often does, damage us as well as others.

Like knives, our boundaries can shape or wound, clarify or puncture, sharpen or destroy, our relationships. How they function depends not merely upon how any one person, or nation, intends to use them, but rather upon whether they are formed in the context of mutually empowering relationship, in which together we create boundaries to serve both our common and our different purposes.

My boundaries are not simply mine. They are between us, our boundaries, just as your boundaries are also ours, in the context of our relationship. There is probably no greater relational capacity than to learn, with one another, how to negotiate our boundaries. On this capacity may well depend not only the future of our personal relationships but also the future of our world.

Boundaries vary in shape, strength, and purpose in different relationships and different situations. My sense of the integrity, safety, and desires of my body depends, for example, upon whether I am lying beside my lover in a sunny field, hid from public view, or am walking alone at night through a neighborhood that is strange to me.

Basking together in a warm field can be a highly eroticized experience for those delighted by the mingling of sex and the natural world. Opening me to wildflowers, sun, and to the one beside me, the power of the erotic draws me out, unfolding me more and more, to my partner and our meadowed bed. Our boundaries become fluid, light, easy to move through into one another's bodyselves.

When I walk alone at night through a neighborhood I don't know, especially if I experience myself as "different" from those around me—different race, gender, nationality, language—the erotic is likely to draw me into myself. As protective impulse, she closes me to the immediate sensory apprehension of what is happening around me and enables me to be with myself in a special, immanent way: Centered and tough within the boundaries of my flesh, I become self-contained in the moment.[45] My boundaries become tight, thick, difficult to penetrate.

The erotic blesses us with transcendence and immanence. She enables us to cross boundaries and draws us more fully into ourselves. She compels us to touch one another without fear and allows us to go into ourselves to feel safe. Teaching us a rhythm of transcendence and immanence, of reaching out and going in, of letting go and holding on, she enables us to make love/justice. She teaches us to be friends.

If we are open to the world in which we live, if we are risking and changing and becoming ourselves in relation, our boundaries will not be rigid *because* we are growing. In the erotic dance of transcendence, they will enable us to create resting places among ourselves and find peace within ourselves as well.

And how might we envision ourselves embodying transcendence? Are there images, memories, links with our past/future, to help us envision more vividly the spiritual shape of ourselves in relation? Are there ways of picturing ourselves collectively that may help us imagine the extent to which we are responsible, with one another, for our mutual well-being—for the well-being, that is, of our whole body?

In the lenten (christian) season of 1984, *Christa*—a bronze crucifix of a female Christ by British sculptor Edwina Sandys—was displayed in New York's Cathedral of St. John the Divine. This image of redemptive womanpower generated quite a stir among good christian folk.

Christa is a controversial concept. She represents an embodied energy that, if released among us, will change the world. Among progressive christians, there is nothing especially alarming about the religious mandate to change the world, a goal easily affirmed because it seems safely remote from our daily lives. In the context of sexist, erotophobic patriarchy, Christa, unlike the male Christ, is controversial because her body signals a crying need for woman-affirming (nonsexist), erotic (nonerotophobic) power that, insofar as we share it, will transform a world that includes our own most personal lives in relation.

Historically, the male Christ has symbolized the extent to which good (christian) men, and women who aspire to be like them spiritually, will suffer and, if need be, die for their faith in a god whose very being is antithetical to eros, to women, and, most definitely, to erotic women. As Mary Daly notes, christianity has become, over its two millennia, a necrophilial religion centered around a dead man.[46]

Because the church has established itself as a custodian of misogynist, erotophobic theological values, the body of Christ is losing its appeal for many faithful churchwomen. It is a dying symbol for some women because we are beginning to understand that it signifies death to eros, death to women, and violent death to erotically empowering women who touch one another's lives deeply.

It is imperative that we not glorify the suffering of women the way the church has glorified the suffering of Christ—of all who follow him, and of all who do not. A number of christian feminists have voiced this concern about Christa, fearing that, like Christ, she can represent nothing other than the glorification of suffering and death—in this case, women's suffering and death—as, in some macabre way, redemptive.

In the context of a fiercely misogynist, erotophobic spirituality, however, even suffering women cannot be redemptive. Thus Christa cannot be interpreted merely as a perpetual victim who eternally must suffer and die in order to liberate anyone, including herself. On the church's historical terms, the power of either eros or women can be interpreted only as perverse, never as redemptive.

Yet, Christa possibly *can* represent our creativity/liberation, by becoming a symbol of our predicament, including our need for liberation. Christa can represent the very antithesis of what, historically, the church has taught about eros, women, and especially erotically empowered/empowering women. Christa can signal the opposite of what the church has taught, preached, and (dis)embodied in relation to women and sexuality. She can represent for christian women precisely what the church has crucified with a vengeance, and what we must now raise up in our lives: *the erotic as power and the love of God as embodied by erotically empowered women.* For whereas the suffering and death of Christ has signaled the woman-induced, sexual sin of the world over and against men of God, the suffering and death of Christa, in fact, can represent the sin of churchmen—men of God—over and against women and our sacred/erotic power in relation.

Christa perhaps can touch many christian women at embodied spiritual depths that Christ cannot, because he has become a living symbol of our humiliation, suffering, and death at the hands of christian men. Christa can reflect this humiliation as being specifically the result of men's sin against women. She can signal the need for our resistance.

Unlike church fathers, we must keep our religious symbols open to processes of transformation that will do justice not only to movement in our own lives, but also to those whom we may not know, or may forget, in our generation. Unlike Christ, therefore, Christa should not become the image of any *one* woman, nor of women *only*, nor only of *christian* women and men, nor even only of *human* creatures. It is for this reason, I suspect, that Rita Nakashima Brock speaks not simply of "Christa" but rather of "Christa/community" as "the revelatory and redemptive witness of God/dess's work in history . . . the church's imaginative witness to its experiences of brokenness and sacredness of erotic power in human existence."[47]

Like all religious symbols, Christa should always be transitional—an image to help keep us open and growing in our respect and love for erotically empowering women and men. We cannot get stuck on her as *the* redemptive image, even for those of us who are christians. To reify any one symbol is to give ourselves permission to stop growing and changing.

Christa is no one among us and never will be. She is no one child, woman, or man. She is no one earthcreature, seacreature, skycreature. She moves among us in our right relatedness, the power in our connectedness. Her name can be a christian way of naming the power in relation that is, by no means, a uniquely christian power/God. Hers can be a christian name for eros, the power by which we know ourselves to be a commonpeople.

And while female images of sacred power will always be important for us, none, including Christa, can ever be more than a transitional image for christians. Perhaps Christa can help us envision and embody the sacred/erotic power, which is really our *christic* (fully human, fully divine, fully creaturely, fully creative) power. Perhaps she can help us realize that our christic power is the same *dunamis* that was active in the life of Jesus and in the lives of all who participate in mutually empowering relationships.

As a christian symbol, it may be that Christa can live in continuity with the relational nuances of the Jesus story and with those people, processes, and moments in christian history that have borne witness to, and passed on, our power in mutual relation. But if she is to help us, Christa must be experienced in radical discontinuity with christianity's foundational antipathy toward women, sexuality, and, most of all, toward erotically empowered/empowering women.

When we are most genuinely in touch with one another and most respectful of our differences, we most fully embody Christa. As members of her sacred body, we give and receive power to bless, to touch, and to heal one another, we who are lovers and friends, sisters and brothers, of all creatures and of the earth, our common home. How we do this, how we bless, touch, and heal, how we love and befriend, these are ethical inquiries that move us into the last chapter of this book.

We must keep in mind as we go, now and forevermore, that the body of Christa cannot be, and should never become, an exclusively or uniquely christian body. Hers can be merely a christian name for the universal body of diverse peoples, religions, nations, and species-beings being formed and re-formed by the sacred and erotic power of mutual relation. That we are who we are is more important than whether we name ourselves "Christa" or identify ourselves as "christian."

Speaking for myself, there is no greater delight than to celebrate and share the body of Christa as eternal resource of nourishment on the sacred journey toward justice: I praise her as both ground and figure of our lovemaking. She is in the power between us, in our relation, as well as in the persons we are and are becoming, you and I, together. I see her in you, and I enjoy her in myself. I take her and stroke her playfully. I look upon her with immense tenderness. I take her and nibble a little. I take her and eat, take her and drink. I am taken, grasped, and caressed by her power moving between us. Immersing myself in you, with you, through you, I move with you in the sensual wellsprings of her love. I move with you in the turbulence of her passion.

Chapter 7

UNDYING EROTIC FRIENDSHIP:
FOUNDATIONS FOR SEXUAL ETHICS

"Here, she said, "in this here place, we flesh; flesh that weeps, laughs; flesh that dances on bare feet in grass. Love it. Love it hard. Yonder they do not love your flesh. They despise it. They don't love your eyes; they'd just as soon pick em out. No more do they love the skin on your back. Yonder they flay it. And O my people, they do not love your hands. Those they only use, tie, bind, chop off and leave empty. Love your hands! Love them. Raise them up and kiss them. Touch others with them, pat them together, stroke them on your face 'cause they don't love that either. You got to love it, you! . . . This is flesh I'm talking about here. Flesh that needs to be loved."

—"BABY SUGGS" IN TONI MORRISON'S *BELOVED**

Affirming my sexual and affectional love for another woman profoundly changed how I felt about and lived in relation with myself, calling forth in me for the first time a deep, authentic self-loving. My relational priorities became more intentionally and explicitly committed with women, more radically and deliberately woman-identified and feminist. In coming out, I came home, responding to the "homesick" feeling for myself, women, and an understanding of the Sacred as Goddess.

Eight years later, I am still coming out and discovering its deeper, more radical implications. As I explore a formal return to Judaism, I do so as an openly lesbian feminist Jew. I am more "out" than at any time in the past eight years, more at home with myself, more willing to take the risks that come with coming out as a lesbian woman. My love for and commitment with women in relation has come to call me to an ever more radical justice praxis.

Hannah, theological student

---

* Toni Morrison, *Beloved* (New York: New American Library/Plume Fiction, 1987), 88.

From liberation theology, I have assimilated the powerful image of the Exodus. God calls the oppressed out of bondage; which means God calls gay men and lesbians out of the closet, in order to resist oppression and heterosexism. Coming out is an act of holy resistance. From process theology, I take the concept of how God relates to us—not through force or coercion, but by coaxing, inviting, holding up wonderful new possibilities—seducing us. The urge to come out, to overcome oppression and self-loathing, to celebrate who I am, is the siren call of God, the Divine Lover—the most promiscuous of all lovers.

I believe that for gay men, as for most women, the original sin is not pride but shame. The way of salvation, then, the overcoming of sin, is through pride. It is no accident that we call what we celebrate in June "Gay Pride Week." To be able to say "I'm gay and I'm proud" is a salvific act, overcoming one's own sin of shame, and resisting the external sin of oppression. A Gay Pride march commemorates not only the Stonewall Uprising, but the Exodus.

Robert Williams,*
theological student

T he need for ethics arises whenever, on the basis of our values, we are pulled between conflicting obligations or moral claims.¹ We may value, for example, the commongood of the nation. On this basis, we may believe that we are obligated to pay taxes. However, on the basis of the same value—because we value our commongood as a nation—we may believe that we are obligated not to pay taxes.

We may value the erotic as sacred power. On the basis of this value, we may believe ourselves obligated to reserve expression of our erotic power in its most fully embodied way in relation to one

---

* Robert Williams requests that he be acknowledged for his words. It is important to him that he not make this statement anonymously.

person—our partner, spouse, or lover. We commonly refer to this obligation as monogamy (which means, literally, "once married").

Because we value the erotic as sacred power, however, we may believe that we are not obligated to withhold expression of this power in relation to those friends with whom we are most mutually involved. While we may not be monogamous, we may resist the pejorative connotations of promiscuity that originate in a culture of sex-negative moralism. We may prefer to think of ourselves as open to sexual friendships.

Yet again, on the basis of our belief that erotic power is sacred, we may believe ourselves obligated to reserve the full physical expression of this power in all of our relationships, in which case we may be celibate.

Ethics can help us decide which option may be right for us. We need sexual ethics. We need an ethical, or moral, apprehension of ourselves in relation that can inform our sexual behavior by helping us understand what is right or wrong for us.

This ethical need may be especially urgent today, in a social order characterized increasingly by tales of vicious sexual abuse and, *in a nonanalagous way*, in a historical moment marked by the AIDS crisis, in which even the most loving sexual acts may be the vehicle of a life-threatening virus.[2]

The christian church's flagrantly proscriptive attitude toward sexuality has impeded the possibility even of imagining a creative/liberating sexual ethic among christians. This has been so much the case that today we face a formidable ethical challenge. The task pulls practicing christians and others whose values have been framed within patriarchal religious cultures into wrestling at the core of our life together in an attempt to apprehend the moral nuances of our creative/liberating relational power. As a people, we share the task of constructing sexual ethics that can do justice to our common body by enabling our relational pleasure and protecting us from both abuse and disease.

A sex-affirming ethic is morally imperative. Only if we know our erotic power as sacred can we imagine, much less embody among ourselves, the transformation of alienated power into right relation. And only insofar as this transformation through and toward mutually empowering relation is growing among us, can we struggle with any hope against the alienation and fear in which both abusive power relations and the AIDS epidemic are secured at this time.

Understanding sexual pleasure as a moral good, an end in itself that needs no higher justification, requires serious moral reflection. In this culture of alienation, our sexuality has been distorted in many ways and is used often to hold abusive power relations in place. I am not affirming or condoning sexual abuse. To the contrary, this book is an effort to indict as evil the alienation in which sexual violence is steeped and to present the erotic as our sacred power in mutual relation, source of our redemption from evil.[3]

When our eroticism is perverse—turned away from its empowering purpose in our lives—sex is dangerous, possessive, and violent. But sex does not have to be abusive to be frightening to us and "dangerous" to our feelings of security and stability and of being more or less in control of ourselves. In the mystery and tensions that help generate sexual pleasure—between self and other, now and later, more active and more passive roles, joy and sadness, holding on and letting go—we may bring one another to the edge of "losing ourselves." Safe in each other's arms, we nonetheless may feel overcome by waves of fear or hatred, sadness or despair, feelings neither necessarily at our partners nor at ourselves but rather at whatever may have been awakened in our erotic vulnerability. Such feelings may give us intimations of a god who moves with us in the valleys of the shadow of fear and confusion and death.

Celebrating sex as fun and good is not only important. It can be deadly in the context of AIDS, a pandemic disease, which is threatening and taking the lives of men, women, and children throughout the world. This crisis, we need to be clear, is not simply a biological or medical one, in which the enemy is merely a virus transmitted through blood and body fluids. Nor is the challenge simply to find its cure. AIDS is a socially constructed disease with a number of interstructured foundations: the enigmatic biological character of the virus itself; the politics and economics of the disease (who gets it? what is being done to stop it? what is its cost, and to whom?); and public ignorance of, and misinformation about, the virus (what are its symptoms? how does it spread? who is most likely to get it?).[4]

Other foundations of AIDS's social character include the homophobia-incited propaganda that it is a "gay disease" that has its origins among gaymen and for which gaymen are responsible; and the ignorance and indifference of many leaders in our political and medical establishments to the global character of the AIDS crisis—for example, its widespread devastation among heterosexual women and men in Zambia and among prostitutes who serve U.S. soldiers in the Philippines.

Racism, heterosexism, and other structures of alienation in the United States are giving AIDS its local shape. A massive amount of fear, much of it unfounded, has become the primary cause and consequence of the spread of the HIV (human immunodeficiency virus) among us. This fear includes homophobia, of course, but more basically, erotophobia—fear of the erotic. At its spiritual and emotional root, this is fear of one another and of God/our power in right relation.

In the context of mutuality and fidelity to our commitments, it is wonderful to make love, good to touch and rub and lick and suck each other silly; but we are learning we have to be careful. We are learning to protect ourselves and one another. This is a hard lesson for many, coming at just the historical moment in which gaymen in the United States, and to some extent lesbians and heterosexual women and men as well, have been learning to enjoy our bodyselves in a spirit of passionate and unapologetic sexplay. We must be honest and clear about the dangers of sex, be they disease or violence. We also must help each other frame and live a sexual ethics that affirms, rather than denies or attempts to qualify, the value of experiencing and sharing body pleasures.

Sexuality is not only a source of pleasure and danger in our lives. It is a source of relational mystery and yearning between, among, and within us. As sacred power, eros moves from and toward a deep, shared sense of unknownness that we will never move beyond or comprehend completely. We cannot know fully "who we are" sexually because we cannot know fully the power of God. This is why terms such as "sexual orientation," sexual preference," and even "sexuality" are such vapid proximations of the real thing—the experience of touching one another physically, emotionally, and spiritually in such a way that we come together.

Nonalienated sexual lovemaking brings pleasure and delight. It also brings sadness. It brings memories and reminders. It brings feelings of loss and grief and of longing to hold onto an intimacy we cannot finally have, because relational mutuality, the essence of erotic love, is not possessive. The erotic opens us, changes us, and moves us into becoming ever more fully ourselves in relation.

In the praxis of death, in which both alienation and AIDS place us, erotic power moves mysteriously and purposefully among us as alternative to despair: She is the life force contending against the death wished upon us by those who despise us. She is the lovemaking that resists moralism, the friendship that resists rejection. She is faith in the goodness and power of our bodyselves together as resource for healing. She is the energy to move us through our fears toward one another.

Needs

Ethics originates in the matrix of our needs, values, obligations, and visions.[5] Organized religion in general, the christian church in particular, is not simply unhelpful in shaping sexual ethics. Given the misogynist, erotophobic weight of its sexual baggage, which even the most progressive churches have not discarded entirely, christianity is largely a damaging/damaged participant in explorations of sexual ethics. If we choose to work ethically within the framework of christianity, even at its margins, we should be realistic about in what ways history, traditions, doctrines, and practices of the institution can help us shape our moral guidelines.

Christians who are committed to constructing a sexual ethics of liberation and tenderness, of friendship and touching, need to be aware that our religious heritage will serve us primarily as a foil in this particular task. For some issues, such as war and peace, traditional christian teachings can play a more ambivalent, even perhaps creative, role. The shaping of a humane, body-affirming, relational ethics of sexuality, however, is not an enterprise in which traditional christianity has either experience or knowledge. Like all pioneers, we christians who venture into this terrain will do well to stick together, or we most likely shall get lost.

We need sexual ethics because we are in trouble: Our collective body is badly abused and abusive, broken and violent. Even in many of our most loving, profoundly connected relationships, we incur danger of sickness and death.

We need to realize that our body—our common body/the body of Christa—is in serious trouble. This realization pushes us to think ethically on the basis not of who we are "in and of ourselves," but rather of who we are together, in the world and nation, in our work and love, as partners and colleagues, friends and lovers.

We need to know ourselves as a commonpeople. This involves becoming radically aware of our bodyselves-in-relation. The affirmation of ourselves together allows us to envision guidelines for sexual morality in a confidence that our differences need not break our body. We are one body with many members. We are not alike in our cultures, credos, experiences, desires. . . . *We need to respect our differences.*[6]

Seeing ourselves as one body with a common problem sharpens our awareness that it is our brothers, sisters, children, parents, friends, lovers, and we ourselves who are not well. It is not simply "those others." *We need to recognize that all of us need help.*

To image ourselves as a body with AIDS, for example, compels us toward the realization of our "fear of our own mortality, of the unknown, of death, of the other."[7] *We need to feel and acknowledge our fear.*

Insofar as we experience ourselves as one body, we will learn to walk and play and touch and pray together, as friends and companions, on this all too often lonely pilgrimage toward death. *We need to be mutually vulnerable.*[8]

As one people, we see that we are together in our suffering, our dying, and, as important, our living. This can comfort us. *We need to embody the strength of who we are together.*

As a common body, we begin to understand that the goodness of who we are and the rightness of what we do has little to do with the so-called "virtues" of individuals, but rather with the way in which, as a people, we shape and share a commitment to the well-being of us all. We need to move beyond the scholastic understanding of moral "virtue," or goodness, as the self-possession of a (normally male) individual.[9] *Goodness is a gift we share. It comes to us through mutual relation, and we can only have it together.*

Moving beyond the highly individualized and privatized ideal of moral goodness, we need to realize that it is not good for anyone to suffer and die alone. It is not good to be ascetic, stoic, or keep a stiff upper lip in the presence of violence or disease—especially a disease like AIDS, which is being constructed socially to expunge the oppressed.

We have an enemy, but the enemy is not "them," not "those others." The enemy is not people with AIDS, to be sure, but it also is not right-wing, racist, heterosexist christian individuals. We need to see that our enemy is neither "us" nor "them," but rather is the alienated power relations cemented in fear, much of it our own.[10] It is against the alienation that festers between us that we need to contend. This enemy belongs to us all. It is transpersonal in that it affects everyone and cannot be pinned down, permanently, on anyone.

People who know that our lives in relation are violated and diminished by alienation are better able to struggle creatively against its death-dealing impact than those who deny its effects on us and, in so doing, project it onto others, making "them" the enemy. We need to accept the fact that alienation has deformed our lives and recognize that only as a people together can we effectively resist its lethal consequences.

In a foundational, historical sense, the enemy is also impersonal. It has no human face, but many human faces reflect its impersonal chill. Alienated power undercuts our commonlife and sucks our lifeblood in ways those with social privilege often do not recognize. It is hard for economically secure people to see, or believe, that our society is in trouble. We need to believe that, in the praxis of abusive power relations, every one of us individually is in trouble. We are living on time borrowed from the specter of violent death. We almost have to be poor, sick, old, differently abled, gaymen or lesbians, women raising kids alone, or people of color to know for a fact that the social fabric of our life together is rotten.

Those of us emerging from the underside of history today also may fail to see that our problems—be they AIDS, loneliness, gay-bashing, rape, racist violence, or intolerance—are not simply ours, but belong to the whole society, in which the dynamics of alienation set the terms and construct the conditions for who's to live, who's to die, and how.

The fear in which this alienation is fastened, however, is remarkably personal. We feel it and often we know that we do. But we have learned to feel it toward the wrong enemy. *Rather than fearing our alienation from one another, we have learned to fear one another.* This is especially true if we experience others as embodying and calling us toward something we have not known before—something different, something likely to spark the transformation of our feelings, values, commitments, and other aspects of what we have grown accustomed to experiencing simply as "ourselves"—the very substance of our identities. *We need to experience relational transformation in our loving and working.*

A sexual ethic is not generated out of nowhere.[11] We shape it out of values, needs, and obligations, gleaned from experiences, our own and those of others. On the basis of these glimpses and intimations of where we are and where we can go, if we go together, we need to realize ourselves as friends, which is to share a fully present, sensual experience of ourselves in right relation.

In the praxis of death—of alienation and abuse, and of love and

AIDS—we need to embody with one another an ethics of undying erotic friendship.

Values and Obligations

Two values seem to me basic to an ethic of erotic friendship. Each is essential to our moral embodiment as persons in relation. Each is accompanied always by obligations or a set of moral claims we must honor in order to live our values.

The first is the *sacred value of our sensuality, our erotic power, and our unalienated sexuality.* We are embodied bearers of the erotic/God with one another, as she crosses over among us. The Sacred transcends us in our particularities, joining us together, erotically, as one body; in our sexual relationships, as one flesh. Coming together, we participate in one another's lives, and our mutual coinherence is good.

It is good, because our bodies are good.[12] Our sensual stirrings, which release through us the power of the erotic, are the incarnate ground of friendship. Our sexuality—the desire to touch one another, the yearning to express our erotic power in relation—is good, but often it is distorted by the alienated power relations in which we live.

Thus we are obligated to respect our own and others' bodily integrity and to protect, especially, the bodily integrity of children, women, and sexually vulnerable men.

There are three common violations of our bodily integrity: (1) using unequal power to cross the physical boundaries of other people without their desire to be touched sexually, as in rape, molesting of children, and most forms of incest (all forms involving children); (2) disruption of others' senses of personal safety, as in sexual harassment by strangers or by employers, teachers, therapists, others with power-over; and (3) the commoditization of sex, or the daily exploitation of women, children, and often gaymen, black men, and other marginated males in order to maximize profit and personal or professional gain. The media, entertainment, many professions, and sexist customs all present women as sex objects to be admired, manhandled, screwed, accepted, or rejected, depending upon how much our bodies are worth, and to whom.[13] All violations of our bodily integrity are forms of sexual abuse. We are obligated to hold one another accountable for ways in which our lives support the dominant culture of alienated power relations in which this abuse is steeped.

Another of our obligations is to act sexually only in mutual relationships, in which the erotic moves between us to evoke that which is most fully human in each of us. Mutually empowering relationships tap the soulful place in each person in which vulnerability and strength, passion and serenity, are most deeply touched and mingled. To be mutual we do not have to be social equivalents or equals. A man and a woman cannot be, for example, in a sexist social order; nor can a white and a black person be in a racist society. But we can share a commitment to accompany each other toward more fully mutual ways of being together. We can help create the "not yet" by living toward it in anticipatory, daring ways.[14] See chapter 1 for more on mutuality and equality.

The second basic value for sexual ethics is fidelity, or faithfulness, to our commitments.[15] Fidelity is a relational trust. A faithful commitment holds authority in our lives. To be faithful to a relationship is to entrust ourselves, with someone, to a shared commitment.

One of the contributions jewish and christian traditions can make to sexual ethics is an understanding of faithfulness as morally indispensable to the justicemaking/lovemaking that is the business and pleasure of faithful lovers—be they God and Israel, Christ and the church, or human partners. Faithful lovers call forth the best in each other and, in so doing, become a resource of blessing to the world they inhabit.

In order to make love/justice, we must be in right relation with one another, and right/mutual relation requires that we be faithful. This faith involves trusting that each of us is being honest with the other; that each knows and cares about the other on the basis of who she really is, rather than on the basis simply of who we might wish her to be; and that each desires the other's well-being.

Fidelity is tenacious trust in our relational power to strengthen us to move with friends and lovers into new, sometimes fearful, places of intimacy and struggle. Fidelity is our daring to say YES to the power of mutuality in a world, and in relationships, in which it is usually safer to say NO.

To be faithful to our commitments is to honor pledges we have made to certain people or tasks in the course of our love and work. Commitment involves investing ourselves in purposeful ways to particular people or processes. No two commitments are ever entirely the same because no two relationships or occasions for love or work are the same.

Over a year ago, as part of a spiritual pilgrimage, I wrote four "statements of commitment"—to my partner, to a close friend, to my therapist, and to my sister. Each commitment was unique, different from the others, except in a fundamental way: Because all four relationships were in the process of becoming more fully mutual occasions of growth and joy, what Jean Baker Miller calls "zest," all four statements reflected my commitment to mutuality, and to the particular quality of faithfulness required by each relationship as it moved through passages of change and transformation. This little spiritual exercise helped me see the extent to which mutuality requires commitment—purpose; and commitment requires fidelity—trust.

Fidelity requires each person's willingness to be present with the other in working to create a sense of "at-homeness" or "at-easeness" in which, to both or all persons, the relationship feels cared for. The vital work of "taking care of the relationship" requires negotiating the conflicting feelings, needs, desires, and expectations that are present, to some extent, in all relationships. Most of all, taking care of the relationship means building trust in the particular relational process, building honest connections between and among ourselves.

In learning to take care of our relationships with lovers, friends, colleagues, helpers, and those whom we are helping, we are obligated to honor, rather than abuse, one another's feelings. This requires us to be really present, rather than acting out roles we have been socialized, professionalized, or otherwise taught to play. To be really present with another, we must experience ourselves as connected with the other in what the Stone Center names as "mutually empathic and empowering" ways.

Only when we experience such radical mutuality can we "hear one another to speech," which Nelle Morton commends as a radically creative act.[16] We create/liberate one another by cherishing those who entrust themselves to our presence, and also by cherishing ourselves as we are entrusted to them. The process of authentic personal empowerment is never one-way.

To be mutually empathic and empowering is to learn not only how to listen and hear, well and deeply, but also how to speak honestly of ourselves and be heard from the depths of who we are.

To be mutual with one another, we cannot shield our feelings, hide our vulnerability, by turning away from ourselves and focusing entirely on others. We must be real *with* one another, really present: connected in our souls, the places in our bodyselves in which we know ourselves profoundly to be in relation. Referring to relationships in which, for example, many western helping professionals (priests, therapists) believe that, to be ethically responsible, we must elicit emotional candor from others but withhold much of our own, Audre Lorde suggests that we've got it all wrong:

The need for sharing deep feeling is a human need. But within the european-american tradition, this need is satisfied by certain proscribed comings-together. These occasions are almost always characterized by a simultaneous looking away, a pretense of calling them something else, whether a religion . . . or . . . playing doctor. And this misnaming of the need and the deed give rise to that distortion which results in pornography and obscenity—the abuse of feeling.[17]

Lorde notices the abusive connection between our "looking away" from our real feelings and the violence intrinsic to pornographic (anti-erotic) relationships and images.

If this is damaging in professional relationships, how much more so it is between lovers. To be faithful to commitments in our love and work, we are obligated not to lie to one another, not to pretend that what is happening is not "really" happening, not to "look away" and call our feelings by other names.

It often is hard to speak truthfully to one another of our experiences of one another—especially, in an anti-erotic, pornographic culture such as ours—of our genuinely erotic feelings (or lack of feelings) for one another or for others. It can be difficult to share our deepest fears and hurts, anger and doubts, and especially our senses of erotic confusion. It can be hard to speak truthfully of our dreams or our hopes. But to misrepresent our real feelings is to diminish the relationship. It is to break faith with one another.

Relational dishonesty, even the sort of benign lying done under the rubric of professionalism (that is, of not wanting to harm others), can damage our capacity to trust ourselves as well as others. It can weaken our confidence in ourselves, in others, in our creative erotic/relational power—and damage others' capacities to trust us.

Whether in professional or personal situations, right relationship involves being really present. We risk hurting one another and being hurt. But if the risk is not taken, we invariably suffer what Adrienne Rich described as a relational "distortion which results in the abuse of feeling."

And Rich describes feelings that come when we realize that someone we trusted has misrepresented herself to us:

It forces us to reexamine the universe, to question the whole instinct and concept of trust. For a while, we are thrust back onto some bleak, jutting ledge, in a dark pierced by sheets of fire, swept by sheets of rain, in a world before kinship, or naming, or tenderness exist; we are brought close to formlessness.[18]

To be truthful rather than false with one another, we are obligated not to shut out either our own or others' real—honest, trustworthy—relational presence, but rather to call it forth.

Fidelity enables us to wrestle with one another through our mistakes and abuses, trusting that it is seldom too late to make amends.

It is seldom too late to bow humbly with one another in contrition and allow the relationship to mend, change, and move on in ways that will honor, rather than demean, each of us.

Fidelity enables us to restore trust in our relationship, however much pain we may have experienced together. It blesses us with the courage to say YES to the process of relational transformation. We are able, perhaps only very slowly, to let go of our grip on the past and move more openly into the present/future.

Faithful with one another, we are able to share and learn from the relationship as it changes and becomes different than what it was. We will not have known the relationship, or ourselves, before in quite this way. And if we must let a relationship go entirely, fidelity to one another enables us to do so together: to be really present, through the pain, in the ending, rather than hidden from one another in shame, fear, and absence.

An ethic centered in the value of erotic power and relational fidelity embraces sexual pleasure as intrinsically good. The value of sexual pleasure testifies to the more encompassing value of erotic power as sacred. Because this is so, the fact that sex is pleasurable can never be the basis for judging it wrong.

This point must be stressed explicitly because, in our sex-negative culture, "sexual pleasure" has become such a twisted caricature of itself: To the popular imagination, it signals self versus other, body versus spirit, lust versus love. To speak of one's desire for "sexual pleasure" is to invite charges of narcissism, hedonism, and perversion.

The overwhelmingly negative connotations of "sexual pleasure" as dirty and dangerous to human society may remind us of the actua , historical construction of sexual perversion: As a vehicle for misogyny and erotophobic values, western christian culture has distorted radically our capacity to experience, understand, or trust the erotic as a holistic, body-affirming, spiritually empowering, transcendent movement among us.

To pervert is to turn something completely around from itself.

Sexual perversion is the complete twisting, the total misconstruction, of erotic power. Rather than learning deeply within our bodyselves the faithful lesson that our erotic power is the love and power of God, we have learned to believe that our erotic feelings pull us away from God. We have learned that eros lures us away from whatever is spiritually good and morally right. We have learned that erotic feelings and sexual pleasure are sinful, ungodly, unless confined like a wild animal within a tight container in the form of "morality" or "religious teachings."

Fearing the creative/liberating chaos of their own relational/erotic power, the predominantly white, privileged, male architects of western christian history have created anti-erotic—pornographic—religious cultures. They have left us a theological legacy of sexual violence, in which "eroticism" and "sexuality" represent whatever is antispiritual and ungodly, and in which "God" is the chief custodian of anti-erotic, pornographic values.

Our pornographic values include the perpetuation of the dualism between flesh and spirit, between sex and God, and the frequent experiencing of violence and pain as sexually pleasurable. These anti-erotic values include also the exercise of tight, obsessive control of sexuality, which involves the creation of explicitly pornographic subcultures as a way of containing "sexuality" in particular parts of town, in books, on film, in fantasy.

But, most basically, our pornographic values include the castigation of our erotic desires and sexual pleasure as shameful and guilt-producing. We learn to feel and believe that our strong desire for sexual pleasure reflects our selfishness, sin, sickness, or perversion.

How then, in this pornographic climate, can we learn to value erotic and sexual pleasure as an intrinsic good? It is a lesson vital to our apprehension of erotic power as the redemptive love of God. We can learn this embodied experience only by daring to risk becoming faithful friends and lovers who, together, are committed gently, patiently, and playfully to calling one another into being and touching one another into life. In a sexually alienated social order, such a commitment constitutes a revolutionary act.

At the beginning of this chapter, I mentioned monogamy, celibacy, and an openness to sexual relationships with friends (which, for many in sex-negative society, is considered promiscuous) as different ways of embodying our sexual commitments. Whatever ways we may choose to express ourselves sexually, we are obligated to approach each other's lives with a profound sense of tenderness, respect, and openness to learning *with* each other how we might become more faithful friends—in relation not only to each other but to the larger world as well, to helping make it a more just and peaceful resource of pleasure for all living creatures.

We need to be clear that each of these sexual options—monogamy, celibacy, or sexual friendships—can be chosen in alienation or in fidelity. Each has a history of alienation, and each contains seeds of transformation. Here I will examine only briefly the institution of monogamy as an agency of both alienation and liberation.[19]

As a social institution in western patriarchy, monogamy has its historical origins in the rights of (white) men to "have" (possess) one wife, and one wife only. Thus, even though it has been a blatantly sexist and possessive sexual institution, monogamy has benefited women and children historically by providing them some measure of economic security. As their head, the white man legally has been accountable for his family's economic situation. He has been unable simply to walk away from financial obligation to his wife and children. Sexually, monogamy has benefited white women also by protecting them from men other than the husbands to whom they have belonged sexually.

Because monogamy in western culture has such a morally ambiguous history, it would seem to have little to commend it to women (or men) of any color who do not wish to be the possession of anyone and who, moreover, are able to participate (economically, culturally, otherwise) in setting the terms for how they shall relate sexually and with whom.

Still, we may decide to be sexually active in relation to only one person. We may do so because we believe that this is our best means of taking care of the relationship with a person we have come to love in a primary and special way.

The decision to be monogamous—more accurately, the sexual partner of one person—may be an honest way of embodying and sustaining fidelity to the relationship as incarnate/embodied/enfleshed in a unique way.

The decision to share the fullness of erotic power in a single relationship may be our least emotionally confusing way of building, and sustaining, trust in a particular relationship as the locus of what is, for us, an extraordinary, uncommon, experience of erotic power as the love of God.

In these ways, monogamy can be a resource of remarkable relational empowerment.

Monogamy can be also, however, a smokescreen behind which partners, or spouses, shield their real feelings, fears, yearnings, and relational questions. Rather than enabling a constructive evaluation of the relationship, a commitment to monogamy can, and often does, prevent honest engagement, struggle, and growth in a relationship. An unexamined, static commitment to monogamy can become a canopy for unspoken hurt, lies, and, in time, the dissolution of a relationship.

It is possible, of course, to be compulsive in our sexual behavior, driven to have sex with people whether or not we know them, enjoy them, or even experience much pleasure with them. Evidently, it is as possible for us to become addicted to sex as to alcohol, drugs, food, or gambling. But we ought not to confuse sex-addiction (having to have sex; being driven by our genitals; being out of control of our sex lives) with a strong desire for sexual pleasure, and lots of it, with a lover—or lovers.

To be nonmonogamous is not necessarily to be, in the pejorative sense, "promiscuous"—wanton and nondiscriminatory—in our sexual practices and choices of sexual partners. It may be rather a way of participating in the embodied fullness of different special friendships. Gaymen, more than either lesbians or heterosexual persons in our society, seem to have developed ways of being honest and open in relation to two or more lovers over a single period of time. Often, in these cases, a primary commitment to a particular lover is sustained.[20]

I suspect that the difficulties many women have experiencing or even imagining nonmonogamous sexual relating may stem from some of the least secure moments, memories, and facts of our lives as sexual objects in heterosexist, racist patriarchy. Women have not been treated sexually with dignity or real respect by men. In this context, "belonging" to one man, or one person, has provided women with a sense of at least partial protection from everyone except the one to whom we have belonged.

Whether we are married, divorced, or single; lesbian, bisexual, or heterosexual; sexually active or celibate; in our eighties or in our teens, women's erotic expectations have been shaped largely by the assumption that our well-being depends on our belonging to someone else who will take care of us—parent (traditionally, our father), spouse (traditionally, our husband), or God. This, I suspect, continues to be a root of monogamous expectations among many women of all colors in this society.

Fidelity to our primary relational commitments does not require monogamy. But learning to value sexual pleasure as a moral good requires that we be faithful to our commitments. This is always an obligation that involves a willingness to work with our sexual partner, or partners, in creating mutual senses of assurance that our relationships are being cared for. Thus we are obligated to be honest—real—with each other and to honor rather than abuse each other's feelings.

We are obligated also, in our desire for sexual pleasure, to be patient with each other and with ourselves; to recognize that all caring relationships grow and change, and that individually we grow and change in our own ways at various paces; to acknowledge and respect each other's different senses of erotic need and sexual desire; and to help each other learn not to feel shameful or guilty about what we want (or do not want), feel (or do not feel) sexually.

We are obligated to honor and cherish—but not to obey—one another as, together, we learn to share (and therefore really experience) the pleasures and joys of erotic power.

When we are stuck between different experiences of a relationship or different sexual desires, we are obligated to be faithful with one another. We are obligated, that is, to wait with one another in whatever honest ways we can, trusting that, in her own time, the sacred Spirit will bring us into a realization of who we are becoming in relation to one another. For, even now, we are becoming.

All of these values and obligations must be present in an ethic of erotic friendship. We must live them together if, as a society and as individuals, we are to become mutually empowering people.

We need vision to see our way forward to our common body, back to our senses, and home to ourselves.

Vision

At this time in history, when our common body is broken so badly by AIDS and by violence, we are likely to find ourselves wrestling with the specter of death. Death is a passage—into what, we are not sure. But I am confident that the irrepressible love of God, the sacred power of the erotic, does not simply leave us behind at our death. An experience of undying friendship can provide the basis of an eschatology: of how we experience endings.

Closure, termination, and death can be cruel and harsh, unjust and unwelcome. In friendship, however, the end is not final. Friends bear one another up here and now and well into eternity, the realm outside of time as we measure it. This bearing up of one another, the capacity for undying friendship, is our passion: It is what we suffer and celebrate together; it is what we are willing to die for, hence, what we are able to live for. It secures our lovemaking as well as our leavetaking in faith that our story is not over.[21]

The AIDS quilt is a powerful sign of this passion and this faith.

But what does such friendship look like? What characterizes the relational bond among human and other creatures that, without self-righteousness or retribution, can transform forces of rejection, abuse, violence, and death?

Our body of friends manifests at least seven qualities when we are in right relation: *courage, compassion, anger, forgiveness, touching, healing, faith*. These form a character structure of friendship and enable us to see what it means to be friends: how we act, what friendship involves, who we are when we are most fully mutual with one another.

No one can possess or acquire any of these characteristics alone, in and of oneself. None is a virtue. Each is a blessing available to us through the power of mutuality. Each can ground our faith in the sacred power of the erotic to draw us into our capacities to risk befriending. Incorporating our basic erotic values and obligations, each characteristic belongs to an ethic of erotic friendship.

As I move into these pages, particular people spring vividly to mind. These are folks with whom I've explored depths, heights, and nuances of compassion, anger, faith, and other dimensions of our common relational body. They are sisters and brothers with whom I've learned, more and more, what is involved in embodying these characteristics together. In naming these people, I bear witness to the relational foundations of any creative/liberating ethic.

Spirited brother, Karl, *courage* is risk-taking on behalf of friendship. It is daring to venture into places we have not been before or in which we have been afraid and perhaps still are. Courage is the opening of our minds, and hearts, and our bodies to the unknown and to one another. Becoming friends, we learn to stretch the boundaries of what we have believed to be safe. In so doing, we step together into realms of stronger confidence in ourselves and one another.

We have been taught by virtuous men that to be courageous is to rise above relational vulnerability, and that fear is an impediment to courage. But that is not true. In the process of befriending, courage comes through our immersion in places of mutual vulnerability. Exposed to danger or simply to the unknown, we empower one another to take heart, to keep our courage.[22] This we do by standing together.

Unless we know fear, we cannot know the courage it takes to step with one another into places of sadness, anger, or confusion to discover therein something important we have not known before about ourselves, about others, about the world. Only in such places of vulnerability and struggle can we find the strength born always, and only, through the labor of our power in mutual relation.

Encouraged, we are still afraid, embodied bearers of a sensual fear of what may happen if we go forth into the new or through the pain, but also of what may happen if we do not. Either way the dangers for us may be real. We may be frightened of failure or embarrassment, of isolation or loneliness, of opposition or punishment, of rejection or death. Our fear may threaten to consume us. But to deny it will harm us and others by allowing us to confuse dishonesty with personal safety and, in so doing, to stay out of touch with our relational power, one another, and ourselves.

We can transcend fear as it awakens in us, but only together. None of us can come through fear alone. The illusion that we can be alone—more exactly, the delusion that we *are* alone—is the root of our most debilitating fear. This fear assures us falsely that others can never really be there with us; never be real with us; and never accept us, as friends, in the fullness of who we really are.

Friends taste courage when we speak honestly to one another of our fear. I may fear your rejection, or be scared to tell you yet again that we need one another in this world, or I may be frightened simply of scaling granite quarries. And you may be scared to let me know how much you care, or of making a commitment to a justice in which you do not yet believe, or of the risks of stepping off the path you know so well.

We all fear loss, suffering, and especially abuse, betrayal, and unjust death. God knows, if we are wise today, we fear what is happening to our common body—this nation, this world—and to us all, as increasingly our lives and values are crafted out of fascist, isolating, and often very "professionally correct" assumptions.

Fear has been the traditional basis of sexual ethics. Fear should help us frame our ethics—but not the raw fear that is untransformed by right relation. We need, as a cause and consequence of our ethics, fear that is being transformed, through the power of mutual relation, into friendship and justice.

Untransformed fear, which fragments our lives into sad facsimilies of false love and pseudointegrity, need not rule our lives or shape our ethics. As a moral authority, this fear is unreliable because, as an echo of alienated power, it lies to us.[23] Our fear does not tell us that it is less trustworthy than mutuality. It does not remind us that, insofar as we believe in the sacred power of the erotic in our life together, we are learning to transcend fear and to touch the world in transforming ways.

Barbara, bishop with your soul on fire, *compassion* is a way of being in touch with others, a way of being connected. It is our *passion with* one another: "The passion we might feel if we were with our loved ones in a burning house . . . knowing that, while we ourselves want out, there are others whose safety is as important to us as our own."[24] Compassion is a gift of our genuine involvement in one another's lives. It is a radically relational blessing in which we realize that our own best interests and those of others coincide.

The root of compassion is humility. And if our humility is real, it is our embodied knowledge that our lives are connected and that no one of us is more or less human, greater or smaller than another. Humility engenders empathy and tenderness among us and makes possible our emergence as a compassionate people.

The public shape of our compassion is solidarity, standing with those who suffer most severely the effects of abusive power relations. We do not put ourselves above them or beneath them. We do not tell them what's best for them, nor expect them to know what's best for us. We stand with them in mutual relation, trusting that each has something valuable to contribute to all and that, in mutual relation, their well-being and ours are inextricably linked.

Compassion enables us to know deeply the truth that no one is free as long as anyone is in bondage to dynamics of alienated power, so closely are our lives linked. The capacity for compassion is steeped in the realization of how literally true it is that we live together, suffer together, and die together every day, one day at a time.

Compassion is in standing with one another through the hard places, the bleak days and nights of our pain and fear. Standing with me, my friend knows that my particular suffering crosses the boundaries of my bodyself and becomes ours. And we know, my friend and I, that our compassion—our capacity to suffer to-gether—connects us with friends and lovers everywhere.

It is a splendid desire to want to be ourselves, really present, with those who are present with us. This is not a matter of "give and take," not mere reciprocity. It is the desire for relational partici-pation, a longing to coinhere, to be included in a genuinely mutual process. Such inclusion, or participation, is the essence of mu-tuality.

The experience of mutuality can strengthen us also to live proph-etically as enablers of mutuality. To be in solidarity with those who are not standing with us, to advocate the well-being of those who do not like us, to accept as potential friends those who reject us— this unconditional love, with roots in compassion, is an open in-vitation into right relation. In ways often moving and mysterious, the constancy of this openness reflects the grace of God.

Nancy, feisty friend, *anger* is an uneasy feeling for most of us to accept as good, and creative, and liberating, especially if we are christian. Anger is also an indisputably biblical character trait—the predictable response of Jesus, his predecessors, his successors, and his god to unjust power relations among and between them.

We are frightened of our anger at wrong relation insofar as we fear being in right relation with one another. *Our fear of anger is a barometer of how badly we want to be, but are scared of being, in mutual relation.* Our anger at injustice, at the lack of real mutuality in the world and in our daily lives, signals the depth and strength of our desire to be friends.

As we learn together to recognize and share our fear of anger at wrong relation, we learn better how to sustain our anger, and thus how to be more honestly ourselves one day at a time. We are able to live with less tolerance for nonmutual power dynamics. At the same time, we find that we are more at home with ourselves and our feelings, more serenely grounded in our own bodyselves.

I watched a documentary on television not long ago about the escalating crisis in New York's East Harlem among Hispanic IV drug users who are contracting AIDS. The show was alarming. The number of new cases of AIDS among addicts is staggering. What made me angry about this documentary, however, was the attitude of the newsman toward the objects of the report. The distinguished-looking anglo reporter clearly was mystified by why addicts shoot up with dirty needles and don't seem to care whether they contract the HIV virus.

I was furious and ashamed that so many white middle-strata folks assume that our lives are not related to those of others, especially poor people. In fact, we white middle-income people tend to be disembodied—disconnected from ourselves, cut off from sensual and emotional realization of the ways in which our own lives shape and are shaped by this goddamned culture of despair.

No one wants to be an addict. No one chooses to get AIDS. No one seeks to die alone on the streets. The only people who can imagine that there are those who *do* want to die miserable, lonely deaths are people cut off from their own sensual and erotic power— and out of touch with this sacred power in the lives of others as well.

We support this culture of violent alienation and ugly death by our fear-laced failure to realize that men and women shooting up dope in New York City or any other place are not strangers to us. They represent our repressed rage and sense of powerlessness over our relational lives, which are broken and distorted.

Alienation feeds off the suffering of the poor, powerless, and despairing members of our common body. In an alienated situation, there may be nothing left to comfort our sisters and brothers except a dirty needle or a bad screw. This is reality, and it is not just theirs. It is ours.

If we are a commonpeople, we are also an angry people in the sacred tradition of prophets who do not spare us the wrath of a god who hates and rejects our pious blather and empty rituals and who desires one thing only: that we create justice where there is oppression, liberation where there is slavery, and hope where there is despair.

Anger at injustice is essential to sexual ethics because sexual relationships do not occur in social vacuums. Our erotic capacities are formed and deformed by our alienation from one another and from ourselves. It is enormously difficult to make love in contexts of poverty and despair, injustice and fear, but it may be, in a given moment, all that people can do to share even a glimmer of hope.

If we can touch each other tenderly, urgently, pressing our bodies close as sign of our oneness as a people, our sexual love, like a candle, may curse the dark and, like a spark, ignite our imagination.

As friends and lovers, colleagues and companions, we need to be angry that these dynamics of alienation, violence, and abuse distort our relationships and our senses of who we are as individuals. We need first to be clear with ourselves and each other that this is, in fact, the case—and that all of our lives and relationships suffer the effects of abuse, because all are structured in a social order of alienation.

We should not tolerate the unaddressed presence of abusive power relations among us. We ought not blame one another for the origins of emotional, physical, or sexual violence in our lives. None of us, after all, is personally responsible for the roots or the extent of alienation in our midst, even as it affects us in deeply personal ways. Moreover, very few people desire the effects of alienation in their relationships. But all of us support the alienating structure of nonmutual power relations by refusing to challenge their active presence in our love and work.

Insofar as we resist taking critical inventory of ways in which we perpetuate wrong, nonmutual, relationships, we help hold abusive power relations in place. We must hold one another accountable for participating (often because it seems to be the "professional," or "ethical," way to act) in relational dynamics that wound us and others and sap energy from our life together.

My sister, whom I cherish well beyond our fractured bond, *forgiveness* is in the possibility of our reconnecting. It is an empowering response to woundedness and disconnection. It is our release from the stranglehold of the past and from stuckness in feelings of shame or guilt, remorse or resentment.

Over the door of a prison at the outskirts of Managua, Nicaragua, is a sign that reads, "We are here to build the future, not repeat the past."[25] The possibility of forgiveness—of pardoning ourselves as well as others and of allowing ourselves to be forgiven by those whom we have wounded—is rooted in the belief that we need not repeat the past nor shut the door on it.

Forgiveness is not unconditional. It requires that those who have inflicted wounds recognize what they have done and commit themselves to doing it no more. Moreover, it requires that those who have inflicted wounds allow themselves to be accepted, as sisters or brothers, by those whom they have wounded. *On the parts of both or all parties, forgiveness requires a sense of profound humility—a realization that our lives are connected at the root.*

Forgiving ourselves, we are able to participate in relationships that neither replicate nor disregard the mistakes we have made. Forgiving others, we invite them to participate in creating justice among members of our common body. Allowing ourselves to be forgiven by those whom we have hurt, we experience the compassion of God. This sacred power pushes us into startling apprehension of who we can be: who we are when we are rightly related—secure and safe with one another.

We cannot absolve others or allow ourselves to be pardoned by them unless we can forgive ourselves. If we genuinely can forgive—quit blaming—ourselves for having "left undone those things which we ought to have done and [having] done those things which we ought not to have done," we will be able to forgive others. This is because the ability to forgive is a fully human and fully divine capacity—a christic gift—to see our own lives and those of others as connected sturdily at the root of who we are together: an abused and broken body whose members reflect this violence in the ways we live and who desire to live together in a different way.

The violence done to us does not justify our abusive behavior. But the recognition that all of our bodyselves bear scars of a violence that none of us, rightly related, would have chosen can permit us, over time and with one another's help, to release blame from individual perpetrators of abuse—ourselves and others.

Letting go of blame, forgiving others, we are able to take them seriously enough to hold them accountable for what they do or do not do in the present and future. Letting go of blame, pardoning ourselves and allowing ourselves to be pardoned by others, we are able to be held accountable for what we do, or do not do, as persons in relation.

As a common body, we who are attempting to live in new ways and build right relationships know that we are not alone. We are empowered by having been forgiven and joined by others, and we join now in comforting and empowering others. Able to forgive those who have wounded us and to accept the forgiveness of those whom we have wounded, we can turn our attention to the source of abuse—nonmutual power relations—and struggle toward the liberation of our common body, the healing of our common wounds.

We cannot love one another unless we are a forgiving and forgiven people. As we forgive and are forgiven, we become actively loving people—reconnecting where there has been disconnection, reconciling where there has been estrangement, healing where there has been rupture. This is the essence of love, of making right relation, mutual relation.

Without forgiveness at its foundation, a sexual ethic cannot provide adequate guidelines for our decisions and behavior. Real lovemaking, like friendship, depends upon our desire to see and know one another as we really are, in our woundedness, fears, and mistakes as well as in our wholeness, courage, and delights.

When we are really present with someone, we know and are known by this person. We are able to share forgiveness as a mutual blessing and, in so doing, to provide a resting place for one another close to the heart of God.

Often we do not realize exactly what harm has been done to us or what we have done to others, yet we know that something is wrong. Experiencing ourselves as abused and abusive, we are contrite and confused. This is the motive behind the general confession in the tradition of common prayer. Frequently, we are ashamed to confess to others that we are sorry for the pain we have inflicted upon them. Just as often, we are ashamed to ask others to repent the harm they have inflicted upon us.

May the Spirit tend our hearts, strengthening us to reach toward one another. And when the time is right, may she enable us to confess together:

We have hurt each other in ways particular to who we are, ways neither of us knows fully. We have not meant to do this but we have. Might we be standing at the threshold of confessing this with each other, each asking the other to forgive? Asking that the wounds be lifted lightly to the same gods that let us toss the sun back and forth, from your place to mine, and mine to yours? (The crystal balls still bounce sparkling across Jericho Bay; and I scoop them up.) Will you ask me to believe that you did not mean to hurt me? Will you hear my remorse for whatever insensitivities and pain I may have inflicted upon you? Shall we ask, each of us, to help the other bear these wounds until they are healed in ways that we cannot control or know?

As we wind our ways into this relational healing, we will be wiser, you and I. For an unintentional infliction of pain, however fiercely experienced, coupled with remorse and forgiveness, is an empowering and transforming dimension of love.

And if some are not prepared to meet us in this contrition, those who are can help us hold in our souls an openness, a yearning, and a letting go—a faith, a hope, a love—which together form the basis of a capacity to be with those who are not ready to meet us mutually in this way.

In the spirit of forgiveness, the future is always open. This irrepressible blessing draws us into the very essence of that power which is love, which is mutual, which is movement, which is constant, and which is God.

Precious little ones, Robert and Isabel, I pray you will understand this someday: *Touching* is a primary relational need. As a sensual, erotic pleasure, it is a life-affirming dimension of human experience. We need to touch and be touched to survive. We need to be able to touch and be touched without fear of giving or receiving abuse. Touching is not a right. It is privileged relational communication. Together we learn to touch in healing ways.

To be touched and touching in voluntary, tender ways is to experience transcendence. Whether in sex or other forms of emotional, physical, or political movement across boundaries, touching can be the coming of erotic power into a fullness of embodied love and justice.

Through the AIDS crisis, sexual touching has become associated for many with death. In this context, it is enormously important that people help each other learn, carefully and safely, to make connections between erotic and sexual touching and life itself. Gaymen have made movement in this direction in their efforts toward "safer sex" and in strengthening their communities as friends, family, lovers. But sex continues to evoke fear of death among not only gaymen but all who have friends with AIDS and all who enjoy sex ourselves.

The basic connection in AIDS between sex and death is biological, not moral (although sexual choices, in the context of AIDS as elsewhere, are laden with moral meaning). The basic relationship between sex and life is a profoundly sacred and moral connection. The *moral* disconnection between sex and life occurs in abusive relationships, not in loving relationships which often transmit the AIDS virus.

Whether or not we are sexual lovers, we must learn to touch and be touched if we want to respect the needs of our common body. We need to touch and be touched. People with AIDS need to touch and be touched. People without AIDS need to touch and be touched. Children, women, and men need to touch and be touched, caringly and carefully. We need to hold and be held, caressed, comforted, and enjoyed. To touch one another's bodies tenderly and respectfully is a mighty and sacred good. It is foundational to our being fully human. From a christian theological perspective, it is a way of anointing the body of Christa.

In mutually empowering relationships, sexual touching is within the realm of moral possibility. This does not mean that it is always right, or moral, even in the context of mutuality. It does mean that, in good friendship, sex might be right, depending upon how our lives converge in the matrix of our values, needs, obligations, and visions. The matrix is not only ours as individuals. It belongs to our communities of accountability to other friends and loved ones. In this relational context of accountability, sexual ethics can take shape.

Sexual touching is right only when we are faithful to the commitments we have made.

In this context of relational mutuality and fidelity, sex is not only right. It is sacred. It is sacramental, an "outward, visible sign" of the power and love of God.

Sexual touching between mutually empowering friends is right when it is purposeful and intense or when it is simply playful and recreational.

It is right when it involves the partners' willingness to negotiate—decide together—the terms of the relationship, including its explicitly sexual dimensions.

Sex is right when it reflects honestly the changes and movement in the relationship.

In these circumstances, sex is a process of godding, of moving physically, emotionally, and spiritually together into a strengthening of our capacities to respect and delight in ourselves and others. Crossing boundaries erotically in this way can be a fully incarnate experience of transcendence, in which God comes with us, touching and touched in her deepest places.

When we attempt to relate mutually we need fewer rules to inhibit our touching, sexually or otherwise. We need encouragement to feel more deeply—and honestly—the erotic as source of pleasure, joy, and shared commitment to right relation.

In relationships in which a fullness of mutuality is temporarily impossible, those with power-over others have a special responsibility not to abuse the privilege of touching. In such relationships as those between parents and children, counselors and clients, teachers and students, employers and employees, sexual abuse is terribly common. We need to protect one another—everyone, but especially children—from abusive sexual touching.[26]

Jan, soulful *compañera, healing* is a radically mutual adventure, not a one-way process. Our power in mutual relation moves among us, touching us physically. She also touches us in our souls, in which we know most profoundly our connectedness with one another and other earthcreatures. To touch and be touched, physically and soulfully, is to participate in healing not only others but also ourselves.

People with AIDS and their friends bear witness to the mutuality of the healing that is taking place. When many lovers and friends are dying of AIDS, healing is literally happening through the shared experience of a love that does not die. In this crisis, each person touched and touching is being brought into a realm of new life.

A sexual ethic of undying friendship voices an irrepressible and forgiving YES in response to the NO of a menacing virus and a society bound contemptuously by fear. If our common body is to be healed, drawn into new life and hope, we must learn together how to speak this YES.

This learning requires of us a courage that, outside the experience of radical mutuality, we cannot know. We cannot know how utterly dependent we are on the life-affirming presence of our friends in the face of pain and fear, rejection and homophobia, racism and death. This provides a clue as to why people who are aware that they are dying so often see with greater clarity than the rest of us what is really going on among us. What really matters.

AIDS is a socially constructed disease, which in the United States has had free rein among "expendables" in our midst: Haitians, gaymen, and IV drug users. But as important, it is being socially constructed globally in such a way that the poorest nations among us are the most decimated by the disease because they do not have the money to provide, for example, adequate education about the prevention of AIDS or important nutritional resources to strengthen diseased bodies in their struggle to survive.

Healing does not occur in a vacuum. Like all relational acts, it is political, reflecting our use and abuse of power as a common body and as individual members of this body. It is good, but not enough, to anoint suffering friends with touch and the comfort of our presence. Healing, to be a genuinely empowering process, must be sustained by our political commitments.

And what might such healing commitments be?[27] What commitments would contribute to the healing of our common body?

1. A healing commitment to embody respect for all living creatures—and solidarity with persons of color; lesbians and gaymen; the poor among us; differently abled and elderly

people; women and children and all living creatures who suffer abusive power relations.

2. A healing commitment to celebrate friendship rooted and nurtured through the power of the erotic, and to rejoice in relationships of embodied mutual love and pleasure.

3. A healing commitment to fidelity in our friendships and other commitments.

4. A healing commitment not to grant coupling or heterosexual marriage a privileged social status apart from other forms of relational commitment.

5. A healing commitment to affirm safer-sex play among mutually related persons, an affirmation grounded in respect for bodily integrity and in our needs and desires to touch and be touched.

6. A healing commitment to treat childbearing and childrearing as a special covenant, in which children would be wanted and cared for with tenderness and with respect for their bodily integrity.

7. A healing commitment to nonviolent, nonabusive, noncontrolling relationships and to holding one another accountable for our violent, abusive, or controlling behavior.

8. A healing commitment to acknowledge and confess our relational failures, and to learn from our mistakes, including ways in which we ourselves participate in abusive power relations.

9. A healing commitment to be a forgiving and forgiven people.

10. A healing commitment to recognize the plurality of human intimacy needs, to respect our differences, and to learn with one another a greater capacity not merely for tolerance, but for celebration of our differences.

11. A healing commitment to grant sex a blessed place among us, thereby ending our sexually obsessive efforts to control ourselves and others by rigid rules, "ethics," attitudes, and behavior.

12. A healing commitment to the care and respect of not only human beings but other creatures as well.
13. A healing commitment to help one another keep things in perspective, which would generate humor among us and enable us to smile and laugh—not at, but with, one another. In a perceptive and playful, tender and forgiving spirit, we would learn to smile and laugh together.

On the basis of these commitments, as a healed and healing people, we would comprehend the meaning of "serenity," and we would come to know peace.

Bev, beloved friend, I have spoken already of faithfulness, or fidelity, as a basic value for sexual ethics. It seems to me important to bring the book to a close on this note. For *faith* not only is a value that we bring to our ethics. It is a foundation of our common body's well-being, a structure of our character as a people. By faith I do not mean *christian* faith. I mean an affirmative response to eros, our power in mutual relation. For christians and other monotheists, faith in our erotic power as sacred constitutes an affirmative response to the love of God. From a christian perspective, this faith is indispensable to the claims of creation/liberation, to the work of lovemaking/justicemaking in the great and small places of our life together on this planet.

In November 1987, at the end of a presentation I was making on the moral fabric of our lives in this nation, a woman came up to me, reached toward me, put her hands on my shoulders, and spoke with authority:

"Being a black woman in the United States, I *know* that if you don't have faith, you don't survive—faith and a sense of humor. We've got to help each other keep faith. You've helped me today, and I figured that maybe my telling you this would help you."

I was touched by what she said. "Thanks," I responded. "Your voice is the voice of God for me today." And it was.

Faith is the tenacity to keep on believing in the power of mutuality/justice/friendship, despite the NO being spoken, all around and within us, to this radical and sacred possibility.

I believe. Help thou my unbelief.

We may assume that it is impossible, that we cannot transcend the ways we have learned to relate safely, that we cannot go beyond the places we have been already, in which the risks feel minimal and the dangers few. We may feel like it is too late for us, that we cannot change now in such basic ways, that we cannot envision our lives transformed at the root. We may have come to believe that we do not want to be moved so deeply. We may insist that familiar patterns, with minor alterations, will suffice, that they will protect us and others from the possibility of serious harm. For, despite our sacred yearnings, we do not yet believe that love is stronger than fear, or that courage can be forged out of fear and pain.

We may feel compassion toward others, and we may be gentle with ourselves, but we do not yet really believe that this tenderness is the root of the power to change the world, beginning with our own lives. We may experience anger at abuse done to others and to us, but we do not yet believe that this anger is indispensable to the work of love, and that together we can learn creatively how to sustain anger at dynamics of isolation and abuse as they threaten to break our bodies, spirits, and dreams.[28] We may know that we need to forgive and be forgiven, but we do not yet believe that our willingness to share pardon will unlock the door to the fullness of our humanity and release among us the divine spark.

What we want most terrifies us: to be touched and touching in our deepest places, to reach and be reached as undying friends. We believe, yet we do not believe, in the power of the erotic to heal our brokenness and make us whole, bearers with one another of the passionate love of God. We believe, yet we do not believe, in our sacred time together, a matrix of patience and perseverance in which mutuality is being conceived among us and born even now, not in spite of our fears and faithlessness, but through them.

I believe. Help thou my unbelief.

Like a mustard seed, our faith may be tiny and hid deep among us. But it is growing with us if, in the recesses of our imagination, we have been together already, friends and soulmates, sisters and brothers.

Faith is becoming among us if, when we are honest, we know ourselves connected already through our values and visions, our fears, and even the smallest measures of our courage. Faith is being born with us if we see the faintest glimmers of mutuality in our memories, our tenderness, and our anger, in our needs to forgive and be forgiven, to touch and be touched by one another's stories and lives. Faith is growing with us even now through the hurtful ruptures between us that tear at our body and invoke our yearnings for healing, though it is in pain and fear that we have trouble believing in one another, in ourselves, and in the sacred power of our mutual possibilities.

As we see through a glass dimly who we really are, our faith assures us that, whether in this moment we are withholding or pushing, resisting or insisting, shutting out or inviting in, the desire for right relation can provide a sacred passage into itself. For faith transforms longing into divine presence, and what we fear to have been merely a mirage we stumble into at the heart of God: We see ourselves together, created in the image of undying friendship, the dream of a common language, our vision of mutual relation.

I believe. Help thou my unbelief.

For even the smallest portion of faith is seasoning our vulnerability to one another, sharpening our images of mutuality. And a quiet confidence begins to form. Drawing us toward one another, it secures our sensual knowledge of the love of God as our YES to justice and to touching, our YES to standing with and risking with, to sitting with and waiting with, to crying with and praying with, to working with and playing with, our YES to friendship, YES to our undying, and to our healing you and healing me, our YES, O YES.

opening

they are so old and many
the women brown, gray, and wrinkled,
bent and broken   sparkling   spirited
some i recognize   many i don't
and a sprinkling of men   children
other creatures with them
and they gather round me and press
in close   and lay their hands
upon me   and touch me with their cheeks
and paws   and i hear them say
you can draw your strength from us.

years later   bone-tired
of stubborn fears gods
words rules
my own resistance i surrender   *yes.*

open your hands
not to hold but to touch
open your heart
not to take but to meet
you will be my sister   and
you can draw your strength from us.

to A.

NOTES

My thanks beyond words to Ellen Davis and Lisa Hammer for their assistance in researching and writing notes to the introduction and chapters 1 through 5.

Introduction

1. In December 1985, Audre Lorde wrote, "I want to live the rest of my life, however long or short, with as much sweetness as I can decently manage, loving all the people I love, and doing as much as I can of the work I still have to do. I am going to write fire until it comes out of my ears, my eyes, my nose-holes—everywhere. Until it's every breath I breathe. I'm going out like a fucking meteor!" Audre Lorde, *A Burst of Light: Living with Cancer* (Ithaca, NY: Firebrand, 1988), 76–77.

2. I explore the concept of power in right relation more fully in *The Redemption of God: A Theology of Mutual Relation* (Washington, D.C.: University Press of America, 1982). This book is written as a companion piece to and development of *The Redemption of God*.

3. For more on dualisms, see Toinette M. Eugene, "While Love is Unfashionable: An Exploration of Black Spirituality and Sexuality," in *Women's Consciousness, Women's Conscience: A Reader in Feminist Ethics*, edited by Barbara Hilkert Andolsen, Christine E. Gudorf, and Mary D. Pellauer (San Francisco: Harper & Row, 1985), 121–41; James B. Nelson, *Between Two Gardens: Reflections on Sexuality and Religious Experience* (New York: Pilgrim Press, 1983), especially chapters 1, 2, and 9, 3–38, 140–55; and Rosemary Radford Ruether, *Liberation Theology: Human Hope Confronts Christian History and American Power* (New York: Paulist Press, 1972).

4. I was pushed by a group of students, particularly Mykel Johnson, to explore this question. Myke was one of a number of lesbian students who, in a class at the Episcopal Divinity School in the fall of 1988, read this text as it was taking final form. Together we argued, discussed, and questioned this and other texts. The influence of these students is found throughout this book.

5. Marx argued that activity shapes ideas and that ideas are not constants that have existed as constants throughout time. "It is not the consciousness of men that determines their being, but on the contrary, their social being that determines their consciousness." Robert C. Tucker, ed., *The Marx-Engels Reader*, 2d ed. (New York: W. W. Norton, 1978), 3.

   Scholars in the sociology of knowledge used Marx as one of their bases for challenging idealism and the notion that ideas arise out of "nowhere," or simply out of other ideas. See Werner Stark, *The Sociology of Knowledge: An Essay in Aid of a Deeper Understanding of the History of Ideas* (London: Routledge and Kegan Paul, 1958).

   This understanding of the roots of our knowledge is pivotal to the work of such people as Paulo Freire in his book *Pedagogy of the Oppressed*, translated by Myra Bergman Ramos (New York: Herder and Herder, 1970); and in the MudFlower Collective's *God's Fierce Whimsy: Christian Feminism and Theological Education* (New York: Pilgrim Press, 1985). Both Freire and the MudFlower Collective start with the presupposition that knowledge is socially constructed and restricted. It is the business of educators to demystify the usually well-disguised social origins of knowledge and thereby render it accessible to a larger number of people than otherwise would aspire to it.

6. Diane Moore and Gordon Bugbee, Doctor of Ministry students at the Episcopal Divinity School (EDS) and my teaching assistants for an "Introduction to Feminist Liberation Theology" course in Spring 1989, have been instrumental to my deepening understanding of this issue. For more on the effects of the universalization of experience and the need to name our own particularities, see Audre Lorde, "The Transformation of Silence into Language and Action" and "Age, Race, Class and Sex: Women Redefining Difference," in *Sister Outsider: Essays and Speeches* (Trumansburg, NY: Crossing Press, 1984), 40–44 and 114–23, respectively; and Adrienne Rich, "Notes Toward a Politics of Location," in *Blood, Bread and Poetry: Selected Prose 1979–1985* (New York: W.W. Norton, 1986), 210–31. See also Carol S. Robb's discussion of objectivity in "Introduction," in Beverly Wildung Harrison, *Making the Connections: Essays in Feminist Ethics*, edited by Carol S. Robb (Boston: Beacon Press, 1985), xv.

7. "*Somos el Barco*" ("We are the Boat"), words and music by Lorre Wyatt, Roots and Branches Music, Redwood Records, 476 W. MacArthur Blvd., Oakland, CA, 94609.

8. I first met Margaret Huff in 1987 when she taught at EDS. She is a friend and active participant in my work, particularly in making the connections between theology and psychology.

9. The Robert S. and Grace W. Stone Center for Developmental Services and Studies was dedicated at Wellesley College in the fall of 1981. It

   has the unique advantage of immersion in a community of scholars and teachers who can add the broad perspectives of the humanities, sciences and social sciences to the Center's psychological expertise. The Stone Center is developing programs aimed toward the following goals: research in psychological development among people of all ages; service, demonstration and research projects which will enhance psychological development of college students; and service, research and training in the prevention of psychological problems.

Work in Progress (Wellesley: The Stone Center Working Paper Series), inside cover.

10. Object-relations theory is built on the presupposition that the inner workings of the self can be understood only in the context of relation of the object and the self. For more on object-relations theory, see W. Ronald Fairbairn, *An Object Relations Theory of Personality* (New York: Basic Books, 1962); Alice Miller, *For Your Own Good: Hidden Cruelty in Childrearing and the Roots of Violence,* translated by Hildegard and Hunter Hannum, (New York: Farrar, Straus, Giroux, 1983); and Alice Miller, *Thou Shalt Not Be Aware: Society's Betrayal of the Child,* translated by Hildegard and Hunter Hannum (New York: New American Library, 1984); and Donald W. Winnicott, *The Maturational Processes and the Facilitating Environment* (London: Hogarth Press, 1965).

The Stone Center goes further than this theory in suggesting that the relation is not only important for *understanding* the self but for the very *existence* or experience of the self. According to the Stone Center, the self exists only within the relational matrix. Moreover, selves-in-relation are fundamentally co-subjects rather than subject and object. For the Stone Center, unlike object-relations theorists, the primary developmental dynamic and interest is *in the relation* itself as active agency.

11. The concepts of empathy and empowerment are integral to the work being done at the Stone Center. Empowerment is understood to be "the motivation, freedom, and capacity to act purposefully, with the mobilization of the energies, resources, strengths or powers of each person through a mutual, relational process." Janet L. Surrey, Ph.D., "Relationship and Empowerment," *Work In Progress,* no. 30 (Wellesley: The Stone Center Working Paper Series, 1987), 3.

Empathy is defined as

the inner experience of sharing in and comprehending the momentary psychological state of another person. Empathy . . . is a complex process, relying on a high level of psychological development and ego strength. In order to empathize, one must have a well-differentiated sense of self in addition to an appreciation of and sensitivity to the differentness as well as the sameness of another person.

Judith Jordan, "Empathy and the Mother-Daughter Relationship," in "Women and Empathy: Implications for Psychological Development and Psychotherapy," *Work in Progress,* no. 82–02 (Wellesley: The Stone Center Working Paper Series, 1983), 2.

12. Janet Surrey made this comment to me during a conversation about the manuscript of this book in December 1988.

13. Jean Baker Miller, M.D., "What Do We Mean by Relationships?" *Work in Progress,* no. 22 (Wellesley: The Stone Center Working Paper Series, 1986), 3.

14. Martin Buber, *I and Thou,* translated by Walter Kaufman with prologue "I and You" and notes (New York: Charles Scribner's Sons, 1970). Although not the most recent, this translation best captures the full meaning of Buber. Kaufman's translation communicates the interpersonal *and* the social/political implications of this work, both of which were important to Buber.

15. See John Macmurray, *The Self as Agent* (New York: Harper and Brothers, 1957).

16. See Zillah Eisenstein, *The Radical Future of Liberal Feminism* (New York: Longman, 1981); and Sheila Rowbotham, *Hidden from History: Rediscovering Women in History from the 17th Century to the Present* (New York: Vintage Books, 1976), and *Women, Resistance and Revolution: A History of Women Resistance and Revolution in the New World* (New York: Vintage, 1983).

    In addition, Marxian analysis informs the work of some feminist theologians. See, for example, Sheila Briggs, "Images of Women and Jews in Nineteenth- and Twentieth-Century German Theology," in *Immaculate and Powerful: The Female in Sacred Image and Social Reality*, edited by Clarissa W. Atkinson, et al. (Boston: Beacon, 1985), 226–59; Sheila Briggs, "Sexual Justice and the 'Righteousness of God,' " in *Sex and God: Some Varieties of Women's Experience*, edited by Linda Hurcombe (New York: Routledge and Kegan Paul, 1987), 251–77; and Harrison, *Making the Connections*, particularly "The Effect of Industrialization on the Role of Women," 42–53, and "The Role of Social Theory in Religious Social Ethics: Reconsidering the Case for Marxian Political Economy," 54–80.

17. The Stone Center uses the term response/ability to describe the concept that the ability to act comes from within relationship and grows as we respond to each other in relationships. The concept of response/ability also includes "the idea that we each have the responsibility to recognize and attend to the experience of others, to participate in ongoing mutual empathy." Jean Baker Miller, M.D., "What Do We Mean by Relationships?" *Work in Progress*, no. 22 (Wellesley: The Stone Center Working Paper Series, 1986), 14.

18. Elie Wiesel won the Nobel Peace Prize in 1986 for his work as a survivor of the Holocaust committed to the act of remembering the event so that it will not be repeated. Wiesel struggles with theological questions arising from the Holocaust and has insisted that christians be held accountable. His many works include: *Night*, foreword by François Mauriac, translated by Stella Rodway (New York: Avon, 1969); *Dawn*, translated by Frances Frenaye (New York: Avon, 1970); *The Gates of the Forest*, translated by Frances Frenaye (New York: Avon, 1967); *The Town Beyond the Wall*, translated by Stephen Becker (New York: Holt, Rinehart and Winston, 1964). See also Robert McAfee Brown, *Elie Wiesel: Messenger to All Humanity* (Notre Dame: University of Notre Dame Press, 1984).

19. The first and second person imply a dynamic relationship, while the third person is distancing, placing a dispassionate (and false) sense of authorship/ authority. Insofar as my words bear authority, may it be passionate and provocative. Therefore my choice of the first and second person is not just stylistic. It is an attempt to engage you, the reader, in "conversation" about issues of living, dying, loving, and working. My use of the first person plural *we* as primary author/subject of the book runs a risk, I am aware, of being read as a blurring of differences between us. This is not my intention. My purpose is to signal the radicality of the relational matrix in which, literally, I do not exist without you. We are distinct, unique persons. But we are persons, you and I, and our "we-ness" provides the ontological grounding, as well as moral pos-

sibilities, for our infinitely varied and particular experiences of the erotic as power.

1. Coming Out: Coming into Our *YES*

1. Deity is, of course, neither male nor female. But as a christian experiencing the power of relation among, between, and in women, I find it helpful at times to employ Goddess imagery and signal Goddess power as woman power. Joining here with many sisters, I am participating in reclaiming the good, creative, sacred power of woman and woman's erotic power. This power cannot be reduced simply to another face, persona, archetype, or image of jewish and christian deity "God." When I speak of God in this book, I am referring to a sacred source of power, erotic and liberating. Like the christian and jewish deity, this power is committed to right relation/justice; and, like the Goddess, this power is committed also to women, girls, the earth, and many delights. She includes some dominant christian images of God, but is far more delightful, mysterious, and vast.

 Nelle Morton, in her essay "The Goddess as Metaphoric Image," draws metaphors from her own experience of the Goddess that become "exorcisms" of male images from patriarchal religion. Morton implies that the Goddess as metaphor is an internal experience, not "something 'out there' coming in to enlighten" her. Nelle Morton, *The Journey is Home* (Boston: Beacon Press, 1985), 164.

 Carol Christ writes that our symbols and language must reflect a changed imagery: "These three issues—female power, the female body, and finitude—have consistently been denied in western religion and . . . the symbol of the Goddess forces their recognition more clearly than any other symbol." Carol P. Christ, *Laughter of Aphrodite* (San Francisco: Harper & Row, 1987), 156.

2. Paul Tillich's understanding that salvation is incomplete or limited when approached by the "individual in isolation" is an important step toward understanding mutuality and right relation. However, his inability or unwillingness to examine differences in power and privilege of individuals within the community left his concept of ground of being disconnected from the real experience of humanity. In addition, he tended to understand ground of being as fixed, static, and constant rather than moving, flowing, and changing with the changes in community. Paul Tillich, *Systematic Theology: Vol. I* (Chicago: University of Chicago Press, 1951), 147.

3. In a conversation in April 1989, Beverly Harrison defined advanced patriarchal capitalism as "corporate monopoly capitalism, in which monopolizing the modes of production is the sole aim of the economic system. The system is patriarchal in that it perpetuates patterns of male domination beyond the family into the realm of political economy."

4. As will become evident, I am heavily dependent in this book on the work of Audre Lorde, especially her 1978 essay, "Uses of the Erotic: The Erotic as Power." Audre Lorde speaks of the erotic as an "assertion of the life force of women; of that creative energy empowered." She writes that our knowledge of

the erotic is a bridge between the spiritual and political split of our society; the erotic lessens the "threat" of difference and acts as a basis for understanding. Being in touch with the erotic motivates action against oppression from a deep, empowered place within. Audre Lorde, *Sister Outsider: Essays and Speeches* (Trumansburg, NY: Crossing Press, 1984), 55.

It is important, and troubling to me, to note the difficulties women have had in affirming Lorde's remarkable insights in her work on the erotic. In an interview with Adrienne Rich, Lorde says,

I address this at the very beginning: I try to say that the erotic has been used against us, even the word itself, so often, that we have been taught to suspect what is deepest in ourselves, and that is the way we learn to testify against ourselves, against our feelings. When we talk in terms of our lives and our survival as women, we can use our knowledge of the erotic creatively. The way you get people to testify against themselves is not to have police tactics and oppressive techniques. What you do is to build it in so people learn to distrust everything in themselves that has not been sanctioned, to reject what is most creative in themselves to begin with, so you don't even need to stamp it out. A Black woman devaluating another Black woman's work. The Black women buying that hot comb and putting it in my locker at the library. It wasn't even Black men; it was Black women testifying against ourselves. This turning away from the erotic on the part of some of our best minds, our most creative and analytic women, is disturbing and destructive. Because we cannot fight old power in old power terms only. The only way we can do it is by creating another whole structure that touches every aspect of our existence, at the same time as we are resisting.

"An interview: Audre Lorde and Adrienne Rich," in Lorde, *Sister Outsider*, 102–103.

For other feminist theologians on the erotic, see Paula M. Cooey, "The Word Became Flesh: Woman's Body, Language, and Value," in *Embodied Love: Sexuality and Relationship as Feminist Values*, edited by Paula M. Cooey, Sharon A. Farmer, and Mary Ellen Ross (San Francisco: Harper & Row, 1987), 17–33; and Rita Nakashima Brock, *Journeys By Heart: A Christology of Erotic Power* (New York: Crossroad, 1988).

5. Martin Buber, *I and Thou*, translated by Walter Kaufman (New York: Charles Scribner's Sons, 1970), 69.

6. The doctrine of the Trinity is central to classical christian theology. This doctrine states that there is one God of one substance, *homoousios*, yet in three persons, *hypostases*. It is a mystery of faith in that, while not contrary to rational or logical thought, it is not possible to prove or disprove it.

The doctrine of the Trinity was developed by the church fathers in the first five centuries of the Common Era (C.E.), in response to those who wanted to make God the "Father" or Jesus the "Son" or the Holy Spirit superior or inferior to each other. Another concern for these men was to maintain a monotheistic deity while honoring these three understandings of God. The doctrine of the Trinity was also developed to counter those who claimed that Jesus was only divine and those who claimed Jesus was only human.

Fought out by the theological and religious authorities in the fourth and fifth centuries (the doctrine of the Trinity was developed in the Councils of Nicea [325 C.E.] and Chalcedon [451 C.E.]), the winners became church fathers and the losers heretics. This doctrine remains, technically, unchanged to this day and is still affirmed liturgically by many christians, especially in the Apostles and Nicene Creeds.

It was Augustine who began to shape a doctrine of the Trinity that moved from a static icon of divinity to a relational imagery. Augustine saw the Persons of the Trinity "grounded in their mutual relations with the Godhead." "The Spirit . . . is distinguished from Father and Son inasmuch as He is 'bestowed' by Them; He is Their 'common gift,' being a kind of communion of the Father and Son, or else the love which they together pour into our hearts." J. N. D. Kelley, *Early Christian Doctrines* (New York: Harper & Row, 1958), 274. Also, Augustine, *De Trinitate*, translated by Stephen McKenna (Washington: Catholic University of America Press, 1963).

7. Nature feminists have helped change symbols in our society that have been used by the dominating patriarchal system as forms of perpetuating the nature/ history split, symbols that imply power-over both women and nature. In her essay "On Healing the Nature/History Split in Feminist Thought," Joan Griscom discusses the common ground within different feminist organizations that are trying to mend the nature/history split: "Those working to further a religion of ecology, such as feminist Wicca, are seeking symbols that can transform our consciousness and thus our culture." The work of Wicca and other groups that are creating earth-centered images of the divine feminine is being introduced more and more into christian and postchristian feminist writers. Joan Griscom, "On Healing the Nature/History Split in Feminist Thought," in *Women's Consciousness, Women's Conscience: A Reader in Feminist Ethics*, edited by Barbara Hilkert Andolsen, Christine E. Gudorf, and Mary D. Pellauer (San Francisco: Harper & Row, 1985), 87. See also, Starhawk, *Dreaming the Dark: Magic, Sex and Politics* (Boston: Beacon Press, 1982). Even as this book goes to press, an eco-feminism movement is emerging among feminist theological students who are drawing upon such resources as Starhawk; Paula Gunn Allen, *The Sacred Hoop* (Boston: Beacon Press, 1986); and Pam McAllister, ed., *Reweaving the Web of Life: Feminism and Non-Violence* (Philadelphia: New Society Publishers, 1982).

8. Pierre Teilhard de Chardin, *Science and Christ*, translated by R. Hague (New York: Harper & Row, 1965), 12–13.

9. Janet Surrey discusses "mutual empowerment" in a mother-daughter relationship in which "the emotional and cognitive connections based on shared understanding develops over time into a mutual process in which both mothers and daughters become highly responsive to the feeling states of the other." The daughter is learning to "take care of the relationship" by developing "empathetic competence." It is reciprocity of understanding that fosters "real relation." Janet Surrey, "Self-in-Relation: A Theory of Woman's Development," *Work in Progress*, No. 13 (Wellesley: The Stone Center Working Papers, 1985), 5.

10. See Beverly Wildung Harrison, "The Power of Anger in the Work of Love," in *Making the Connections: Essays in Feminist Social Ethics*, edited by Carol S. Robb (Boston: Beacon Press, 1985).

11. Adrienne Rich, "Split at the Roots," in *Nice Jewish Girls: A Lesbian Anthology,* edited by Evelyn Tornton Beck (New York: Crossing Press, 1982), 72.

12. Jean Baker Miller analyzes relationships of "temporary inequality" as socially structured relations, such as the one between parents and children, and teachers and students, as situations "based in service." Service of the "superior" person to the "lesser" is the purpose behind these temporary, unequal relations. The "paramount goal is to end the relationship . . . of inequality." The inequality presupposes a change of power relations at some point in the future. "The period of disparity is meant to be temporary." The "lesser" individual is meant to move out of a position of being served into a fully acting and knowledgeable equal. Jean Baker Miller, M.D., *Toward a New Psychology of Women,* 2d ed. (Boston: Beacon Press, 1986), 4–5. The therapeutic relationship is one of temporary inequality.

13. Lorde, *Sister Outsider,* 57.

2. Notes on Historical Grounding: Beyond Sexual Essentialism

1. Quoted in Jeffrey Weeks, *Sexuality and Its Discontents: Meanings, Myths and Modern Sexualities* (London: Routledge and Kegan Paul, 1985), 44.

   In his *History of Sexuality,* Michel Foucault asks how power has become a factor in sexuality. His understanding of the sexual relation is one in which relations of power are immanent to it. Sexuality is one of the "specific domains formed by relations of power." Rather than acting out of a mutually empowering relation, Foucault accepts that "disequilibriums" are embedded in the sexual relation. Further, a competitive, aim-oriented power relation gives power to some ("men, adults, parents, doctors") and denies it to others ("women, adolescents, children, patients"). Michel Foucault, *History of Sexuality,* vol. I (New York: Vintage, 1978), 94–95, 99.

2. See Glossary, note 9.

3. The body is a site for historical moulding and transformation because sex, far from being resistant to social ordering, seems peculiarly susceptible to it. We know that sex is a vehicle for the expression of a variety of social experiences: of morality, duty, work, habit, tension release, friendship, romance, love, protection, pleasure, utility, power, and sexual difference. Its very plasticity is the source of its historical significance. Sexual behavior would transparently not be possible without physiological sources, but physiology does not supply motives, passion, object choice, or identity. These come from "somewhere else," the domains of social relations and psychic conflict. If this is correct, the body can no longer be seen as a biological given which emits its own meaning. It must be understood instead as an ensemble of potentialities which are given meaning only in society.

   Weeks, *Sexuality and Its Discontents,* 122–23. See also Mario Mieli, *Homosexuality and Liberation: Elements of a Gay Critique,* translated by David Fernbach (London: Gay Men's Press, 1980).

4. Weeks, *Sexuality and Its Discontents,* 8.

5. *Ibid.*

6. *Ibid.* Jeffrey Weeks challenges the idea of a "pre-given essence of sexuality." Weeks understands sexuality to be open, fluid, and flowing, influenced by changing elements in the culture. Sexuality is moved and shaped by a variety of circumstances. A "fixed identity," one that is static and eternal, inhibits this "flow of different forces and influences." Weeks, *Sexuality and Its Discontents,* 121–22. See also Mieli, *Homosexuality and Liberation;* and Beverly Wildung Harrison, "Misogyny and Homophobia: The Unexplored Connections," in *Making the Connections: Essays in Feminist Social Ethics,* edited by Carol S. Robb (Boston: Beacon, 1985).

7. Dorothee Sölle writes, "In German, *phantasie* has a potentially far more positive value than the word "fantasy" has in English. Its meaning includes the dimensions of imagination, inspiration, inventiveness, flexibility, freedom and creativity." Dorothee Sölle, *Beyond Mere Obedience: Reflections on a Christian Ethic for the Future,* translated by Lawrence W. Denef (Minneapolis: Augsburg Publishers, 1970), 10.

8. Further resources that discuss sex, women, and political control are Harrison, "Sexuality and Social Policy," in *Making the Connections,* 83–114; Weeks, "The 'Sexual Revolution' Revisited," in *Sexuality and Its Discontents,* 15–32; and Sheila Briggs, "Sexual Justice and the Righteousness of God," in *Sex and God: Some Varieties of Women's Experience,* edited by Linda Hurcombe (New York: Routledge and Kegan Paul, 1987), 251–77.

9. In the early christian church, sexual dualism intensified to the point that sexuality was hyper-regulated and made permissible only through pure and exclusive love. Samuel Laeuchli writes that it was a conflict won over by "a tipping of the scale so against sexuality that sexuality becomes synonymous with evil. The sexual act becomes abhorrent and people either flee into deserts or write books on the perfection of virginity." Samuel Laeuchli, *Power and Sexuality: The Emergence of Canon Law at the Synod of Elvira* (Philadelphia: Temple University Press, 1972), 103.

   Elaine Pagels discusses the struggle within the church in the first three centuries for control over people. Pagels notes that sexuality is one distinct area of people's lives that the church can regulate, thus regulating their theology and social lives. See Elaine Pagels, *The Gnostic Gospels* (New York: Vintage Books, 1981).

10. Laeuchli, *Power and Sexuality,* 88.

11. *Ibid.,* 112–13.

12. *Ibid.,* 104.

13. Laeuchli notes that the church is still not willing to open the explosive, yet crucial issue of sexuality (114). The Council of Elvira's refusal to confront the issue of sexuality perpetuates its hierarchical, ecclesiastical authority when dealing with contemporary matters of the modern world. The church's refusal to face its antisexual stance keeps it from confronting relational and interactive issues around sexuality. Laeuchli, *Power and Sexuality,* 122–23.

14. Tertullian, quoted in Mary Daly, *The Church and the Second Sex* (New York: Harper & Row, 1968), 45.

15. Examples of canons that expose the antifemale, antisexual, and anti-Semitic characteristic of teachings include the following: Number 72: "If a widow has

intercourse with a man and later marries him, she shall be reconciled to communion after a period of five years, having completed the required penance; if she marries another man, having left the first, she shall not be given communion even at the end." Number 78: "If one of the faithful who is married commits adultery with a Jewish or pagan woman, he shall be cut off, but if someone else exposes him, he can share Sunday communion after five years, having completed the required penance." Laeuchli, *Power and Sexuality*, 134–35.

16. Haunani-Kay Trask, *Eros and Power: The Promise of Feminist Theory* (Philadelphia: University of Pennsylvania Press, 1986), 56.

17. For more on women and poverty, see Caroline Allison, "It's Like Holding the Key to Your Own Jail," in *Women in Namibia* (Geneva: World Council of Churches, 1986); Beverly Bryan, Stella Dadzie, and Suzanne Soate, *The Heart of the Race: Black Women's Lives in Britain* (London: Virago, 1985); Victoria Byerly, *Hard Times Cotton Mill Girls: Personal Histories of Womanhood and Poverty in the South* (Ithaca, NY: ILR Press, 1986); Zilla R. Eisenstein, *Feminism and Sexual Equality: Crisis in Liberal America* (New York: Monthly Review Press, 1984), particularly 114–38; Harrison, *Making the Connections*; Karin Stallord, *et al.*, *Poverty in the American Dream: Women and Children First* (Boston: South End Press, 1983); Soon-Hwa Sun, "Women, Work and Theology in Korea," *Journal of Feminist Studies in Religion* 3, no. 2 (Fall 1987): 125–35; Rosa Dominga Trapasso, "The Feminization of Poverty," *Latinamerica Press* (May 31, 1984): 5.

18. Weeks, *Sexuality and Its Discontents*, 26–27.

19. In his later writings, Sigmund Freud began to see the "sexual instincts" as the "true life-instincts." He began to understand the sexual instincts as an energy that "preserved life itself." This was a major affirmation not only of the life-instinct in human nature, but the life-affirming instinct of sexuality. Sigmund Freud, *Beyond the Pleasure Principle: The Pioneer Study of the Death Instinct in Man*, translated by James Strachey (New York: Bantam, 1959), 74–75, 79.

This was a major shift for Freud, who had earlier considered the sexual instinct to be a death-instinct. The distinction in his theory came about as Freud began to hypothesize on the "ego-instincts," pressured for death, and the "sexual instincts pressured . . . toward a prolongation of life." (78)

20. Herbert Marcuse, *Eros and Civilization: A Philosophical Inquiry into Freud* (Boston: Beacon, 1955), 201.

21. See Audre Lorde, "Uses of the Erotic: The Erotic as Power," in *Sister Outsider: Essays and Speeches* (Trumansburg, NY: Crossing Press, 1984), 53–59.

22. Mary Daly and Sarah Bentley Doely were two of the first women to recognize that it was not merely changing male god language or ordaining women into the priesthood that was needed for human liberation. They understood that these issues were symptoms exposing the need for vast structural changes within the church. See Mary Daly, *The Church and the Second Sex*; and Sarah Bentley Doely, *Women's Liberation and the Church* (New York: Association Press, 1970).

Radical christian feminists are continuing to explore and expand on the ideas put forth in the above-mentioned texts. See, for example, Elisabeth Schüssler-

Fiorenza, *In Memory of Her* (New York: Crossroad-Seabury Press, 1983); Rosemary Radford Reuther, *Sexism and God-Talk: Toward a Feminist Theology* (Boston: Beacon, 1983); and Harrison, *Making the Connections.*
23. Lorde, "The Transformation of Silence into Language," *Sister Outsider,* 41.

3. Heterosexism: Enforcing White Male Supremacy

1. Adrienne Rich, "Compulsory Heterosexuality and Lesbian Existence," *Blood, Bread and Poetry: Selected Prose, 1979–1985* (New York: W.W. Norton, 1986), 63–64.
2. Mario Mieli, *Homosexuality and Liberation: Elements of a Gay Critique,* translated by David Fernbach (London: Gay Men's Press, 1980), 30–31.
3. I first used this analogy, in detail, in my essay "Can Anglicans be Feminist Liberation Theologians and Still be Anglicans?" in *The Trial of Faith: Theology and the Church Today,* edited by Peter Eaton (West Sussex, Great Britain: Churchman Publishing, 1988), 30–31.
4. Charlie Howard, a twenty-three-year-old gayman, drowned after being beaten and thrown from a bridge by three teenage men in Bangor, Maine, on July 7, 1984. The three men, Shawn Mabry, James Baines, and Daniel Ness, were released without bail to their parents' custody. They were charged as juveniles and pleaded guilty to manslaughter. They were sentenced to indeterminate terms at the Maine Youth Center.
5. For more on Marx and alienation, see Erich Fromm, *Marx's Concept of Man,* with a translation from Marx's *Economic and Philosophical Manuscripts* by T. B. Bottomore (New York: Frederick Ungar, 1961). In his chapter on "Alienation," Fromm states:

> Alienation (or "estrangement") means, for Marx, that man [sic] does *not* experience himself as the acting agent in his grasp of the world, but that the world (nature, others, and he himself) remain alien to him. They stand above and against him as objects, even though they may be objects of his own creation. Alienation is essentially experiencing the world and oneself passively, receptively, as the subject separated from the object. (44)

6. Audre Lorde, "Uses of the Erotic: The Erotic as Power," in *Sister Outsider: Essays and Speeches* (Trumansburg, NY: Crossing Press, 1984), 57.
7. James B. Nelson, *Between Two Gardens: Reflections on Sexuality and Religious Experience* (New York: Pilgrim Press, 1983), 5–6.
8. Beverly Wildung Harrison, *Making the Connections: Essays In Feminist Social Ethics,* edited by Carol S. Robb (Boston: Beacon, 1985), 149.
9. See Marie M. Fortune, *Sexual Violence: The Unmentionable Sin* (New York: Pilgrim Press, 1983), 16–26.
10. *Ibid.,* 27–30.
11. *Ibid.,* 77–79.
12. Harrison, "Misogyny and Homophobia: The Unexplored Connections," in *Making the Connections,* 135–51.

13. Rennie Golden and Sheila Collins, *Struggle Is a Name for Hope* (London: West End Press, 1972).

4. A Sacred Contempt: Heterosexist Theology

1. This chapter is adapted from a panel presentation on Lesbian Feminist Issues in Religion (Women and Religion Section) at the American Academy of Religion, Anaheim, CA, November 25, 1985, and was published in a slightly different form in the *Journal of Feminist Studies in Religion*. See "Heterosexist Theology: Being Above it All," *Journal of Feminist Studies in Religion* 3, no. 1 (Spring 1987): 29–38.

2. For constructive moral epistemologies that build on creative insights from natural law tradition, see Beverly Wildung Harrison, *Making the Connections: Essays in Feminist Social Ethics*, edited by Carol S. Robb (Boston: Beacon, 1985), especially the introduction by Carol Robb and 3–21, 115–34, and 253–63; Anthony Battaglia, *Toward a Reformulation of Natural Law* (New York: Seabury, 1981); Daniel C. Maguire, *The Moral Choice* (New York: Doubleday, 1978); Margaret Farley, "New Patterns of Relationship: Beginnings of a Moral Revolution," in *Woman: New Dimensions*, edited by Walter J. Burghardt (New York: Paulist, 1976); and Barbara Hilkert Andolsen, Christine E. Gudorf, and Mary D. Pellauer, eds., *Women's Consciousness, Women's Conscience* (San Francisco: Harper & Row, 1985), especially 211 ff.

3. See Samuel Laeuchli, *Power and Sexuality: The Emergence of Canon Law at the Synod of Elvira* (Philadelphia: Temple University Press, 1972); Anne Llewellyn Barstow, *Witchcrazed: Persecution by Gender, 1400–1700* (forthcoming); and the classic, infamous, *Malleus Maleficarum (Hammer of Witches)*, translated with introduction by the Rev. Montague Summers (New York: Dover, 1971). Written by monks Sprenger and Kraemer, it is indicative of the extent to which christian assumptions about the natural as moral are steeped in misogyny. See also Harrison on the relation between hatred of women and fear of homosexuality, "Misogyny and Homophobia: The Unexplored Connections," in *Making the Connections*, 135–51.

4. At least one seminary (The Episcopal Seminary in Alexandria, Virginia) requires all of its students to sign a pledge that they will not engage in sexual activity outside of marriage while they are students at the seminary. And at least one psychiatrist who screens candidates for ordination in a liberal Episcopal diocese has indicated to those whom he interviews that their sexual behavior is *the* critical factor in his judging their fitness for ordination. While he expresses interest in hearing details of *heterosexual* lives, he makes no secret of his special disdain for gaymen and lesbians, who in his judgment, as in the judgment of the Episcopal Church at large, are unfit for ordained ministry.

5. For attention to interiorized spirituality as a moral problem, see Dorothee Sölle and Shirley A. Cloyes, *To Work and to Love: A Theology of Creation* (Philadelphia: Fortress, 1984), as well as other pieces by Sölle. This same theme is explored in the Amanecida Collective's *Revolutionary Forgiveness: Feminist Reflections on Nicaragua* (Maryknoll, NY: Orbis, 1987); Gustavo Gutierrez, *The*

Power of the Poor in History, translated by Robert Barr (Maryknoll, NY: Orbis, 1983); and Phillip Berryman, *The Religious Roots of Rebellion: Christians in Central American Revolution* (Maryknoll, NY: Orbis, 1984). In her essay "While Love is Unfashionable: An Exploration of Black Spirituality and Sexuality," in Andolsen, *et al.*, *Women's Consciousness, Women's Conscience*, 121–41, Toinette M. Eugene examines connections between justice, sexuality, and spirituality in black experience.

6. Hannah Tillich, *From Time to Time* (New York: Stein and Day, 1973), 15. I am grateful to Tom F. Driver for reminding me how vividly Hannah Tillich writes of her husband's liberal disposition.

7. See Paul Tillich, *Systematic Theology*, 3 vols. (Chicago: University of Chicago Press, 1951), 2, especially 155–58.

8. *Ibid.*, 2, 52.

9. *Ibid.*, 1, 182–86 on "freedom and destiny"; 1, 255–56 and 2, 29 ff on "the Fall." Also *The Courage to Be* (New Haven: Yale University Press, 1952), and *Love, Power and Justice* (New York: Oxford University Press, 1954).

10. Norene M. Carter, a feminist ethicist who lives and works in the Boston area, discusses Marx's and Tillich's different understandings of alienation in an unpublished essay she wrote for Elisabeth Schüssler-Fiorenza and Carter Heyward's class, "The Bible and Feminist Hermeneutics," Episcopal Divinity School, spring 1985.

11. Tillich discusses "God above God" in *The Courage to Be*.

12. Paul Tillich, *Systematic Theology*, 2, especially Pt. 2.B, 118–24.

13. *Ibid.*, 2, especially Pt. 2.E, 165–79.

14. *Ibid.*, 2, 177.

15. *Ibid.*, 2, 178.

16. Paul Tillich, *Love, Power and Justice*, 70.

17. Friedrich Schleiermacher, *The Christian Faith*, edited by H. R. Mackintosh and J. S. Stewart, translation of 2d German edition (Philadelphia: Fortress, 1976), 332, 335.

18. This is the position of many gay advocacy groups in religion. Alternatives to this theology are being given voice by such gay/lesbian activists as David Fernbach, *The Spiral Path: A Gay Contribution to Human Survival* (Boston: Alyson, 1981); Mary E. Hunt, *Fierce Tenderness: Toward a Feminist Theology of Friendship* (San Francisco: Harper & Row, forthcoming 1990), and Cherríe Moraga, *Loving in the War Years* (Boston: South End Press, 1983).

19. See James Luther Adams, *On Being Human Religiously*, edited by Max L. Stackhouse (Boston: Beacon, 1976), especially 1–88; and Harrison, *Making the Connections*, 81–190, for interpretations of "freedom" and "rights" on the normative basis of justice.

20. See Alison M. Jaggar, *Feminist Politics and Human Nature* (Totowa, NJ: Rowman and Allanheld, 1983), especially 27–50 and 173–206.

21. Important resources for grasping the extent of misogyny—and women's courage and creativity—in christian tradition include Kari Borreson, *Subordination and Equivalence: The Nature and Role of Women in Augustine and Thomas Aquinas* (Washington, D.C.: University Press of America, 1981); Rosemary R. Ruether and Eleanor McLaughlin, *Women of Spirit: Female Leadership in the Jewish*

and Christian Traditions (New York: Simon and Schuster, 1979); Elizabeth A. Clark, *Jerome, Chrysostom and Friends: Essays and Translations* (New York: Edwin Mellen Press, 1979); Elisabeth Schüssler-Fiorenza, *In Memory of Her: A Feminist Reconstruction of Christian Origins* (New York: Crossroad Press, 1983); Phyllis Trible, *Texts of Terror: Literary-Feminist Readings of Biblical Narratives* (Philadelphia: Fortress, 1984). See Clarissa W. Atkinson, Constance H. Buchanan, and Margaret R. Miles, eds., *Immaculate and Powerful: The Female in Sacred Image and Social Reality* (Boston: Beacon, 1985), for similar themes within and beyond jewish and christian religions.

22. It is interesting to me that in Thomist theology (in which the spiritual is the *super*natural and the "male principle" is in its image, femaleness is cast as "natural." But in modern liberalism's equation of the natural with the divine process, the construct of female "nature" (receptive, passive) is set as different from the male "nature," which is normative for a fully human life. Femaleness is thus "unnatural" in liberal theology, as are sexual acts that run contrary to human (and divine) "nature." Whether "natural" (beneath the supernatural God-man) or "unnatural" (beneath the natural God-man), women are objects rather than subjects of moral agency in christian history. Liberalism thus has changed nothing with regard to classical christianity's sacred contempt for women. Homosexual men, of course, have a very different history. As long as they have been "discreet," they have maintained heterosexist benefits of male privilege and domination. Openly gay men—not closeted homosexuals—receive scorn and contempt in christian history.

23. For help in understanding the politics of this dynamic, see Zillah R. Eisenstein, *The Radical Future of Liberal Feminism* (New York: Longman, 1981); Beverly Wildung Harrison, *Our Right to Choose: Toward a New Ethic of Abortion* (Boston: Beacon, 1983); and Jaggar, *Feminist Politics and Human Nature.*

24. John Boswell explores this in *Christianity, Social Tolerance and Homosexuality: Gay People in Western Europe from the Beginning of the Christian Era to the Fourteenth Century* (Chicago: University of Chicago Press, 1980).

5. Authority and Scripture: That Which Can Be Trusted

1. I'm sorry to say I don't remember who told me this story. It was previously published in my book *Our Passion for Justice* (New York: Pilgrim Press, 1984), 183.

2. Avery Dulles, S.J., "The Authority of Scripture: A Catholic Perspective," in *Scripture in the Jewish and Christian Traditions: Authority, Interpretation and Relevance*, edited by Frederick E. Greenspahn (Nashville: Abingdon, 1982), 14.

3. Hannah Arendt, *Between Past and Future: Eight Exercises in Political Thought* (New York: Viking, 1968).

4. John E. Skinner, *The Meaning of Authority* (Washington, D.C.: University Press of America, 1983).

5. Skinner, *The Meaning of Authority*, and Arendt, *Between Past and Future.*

6. *Dunamis* is the Greek word for power. In the New Testament it is used in

contrast to the word *exousia*, which is Greek for authority. Jesus had power rather than authority in the eyes of the religious and secular leaders of his time. For more on *dunamis* and *exousia*, see Isabel Carter Heyward, *The Redemption of God: A Theology of Mutual Relation* (Washington, D.C.: University Press of America, 1982), especially 40–49.

7. Dorothee Sölle, *Christ the Representative: An Essay in Theology after the 'Death of God'* (Philadelphia: Fortress, 1967).

8. Dorothee Sölle, *Beyond Mere Obedience: Reflections on a Christian Ethic for the Future*, translated by Lawrence W. Denef (Minneapolis: Augsburg, 1970).

9. The understanding of God as both the act of justicemaking and those involved in the struggle is found throughout Sölle's work. See, for example, Dorothee Sölle and Shirley A. Cloyes, *To Work is to Love: A Theology of Creation* (Philadelphia: Fortress, 1984) and Dorothee Sölle, *Death by Bread Alone: Texts and Reflections on Religious Experience*, translated by David L. Scheidt (Philadelphia: Fortress, 1978).

10. See Avery Dulles, S.J., "The Authority of Scripture: A Catholic Perspective," and John H. Gerstner, "A Protestant View of Biblical Authority," in Greenspahn, *Scripture in the Jewish and Christian Traditions*.

11. Richard Hooker, *Of the Laws of Ecclesiastical Polity* (abridged edition), edited by A. S. McGrade and Brian Vickers (New York: St. Martins Press, 1975), book 2, chapter 1, section 4, 172.

12. Hooker, *Of the Laws of Ecclesiastical Polity*, book 3, chapter 8, section 18, 207.

13. Resources that deal with reading and hearing the christian bible as *a* word of God include Elisabeth Schüssler-Fiorenza, *Bread Not Stone: The Challenge of Feminist Biblical Interpretation* (Boston: Beacon, 1984), and *In Memory of Her: A Feminist Reconstruction of Christian Origins* (New York: Edwin Mellen Press, 1979); Norman K. Gottwald, ed., *The Bible and Liberation: Political and Social Hermeneutics* (New York: Orbis, 1983); Letty M. Russell, ed., *Feminist Interpretation of the Bible*; and Jon Sobrino, S.J., *Christology at the Crossroads: A Latin American Approach*, translated by John Drury (Maryknoll, NY: Orbis, 1976).

14. Schüssler-Fiorenza, *Bread Not Stone*, xxii.

15. Alison Cheek, sister priest, friend, and Doctor of Ministry student at Episcopal Divinity School, is developing this theme of "historical imagination" through her work with Elisabeth Schüssler-Fiorenza.

16. Alice Walker, *The Color Purple* (New York: Harcourt Brace Jovanovich, 1982).

17. Gloria Naylor, *Linden Hills* (New York: Ticknor and Fields, 1985).

6. The Erotic as Power: Sexual Theology

1. Few christian scholars would dispute the oppositional character of spirituality and sexuality in early christian history, though a number suggest that the early christian understanding of the body was not entirely negative, nor, perhaps, the attitude toward sexual pleasure wholly prescriptive. See Margaret R. Miles, *Augustine on the Body* (Missoula, MT: Scholars Press, 1979), and *Fullness of*

Life: Historical Foundations for a New Asceticism (Philadelphia: Westminster, 1981); also Peter R. L. Brown, *The Body and Society: Men, Women and Sexual Renunciation* (New York: Columbia University Press, 1988); and Elaine Pagels, *Adam, Eve and the Serpent* (New York: Random House, 1988).

2. Margaret R. Miles attributes Augustine's attitude toward sexuality as a positive response to his "sex-addiction": "We must accept Augustine's evaluation of himself as addicted to sex, from which, he tells us, no friendship was free. . . . Augustine knew himself to be addicted to sex, and the resolution of this by the decision for celibacy was not a solution that he urged for anyone else not similarly addicted. His decision was a 'gift of God,' not the result of repression." Miles, *Fullness of Life*, 77.

   Elsewhere, acknowledging the proscriptive effects of Augustine's teachings on sexuality, Miles writes, "[Augustine's] experience was unfortunate, not only for himself, but . . . for all of us who have inherited the effective history of Augustine's ideas of sex." Response to Peter Brown's paper "Augustine and Sexuality" in *Colloquy 46* (Berkeley, CA: The Center for Hermeneutical Studies in Hellenistic and Modern Culture, 1983), 19.

   The fact is, regardless of why Augustine adopted a negative view of sexuality, his experiential and conceptual association of sexuality and sin became the foundation of sexual ethics in western Christianity. I interpret both Augustine's problem and the church's teachings on sexuality to be steeped in a patriarchal, androcentric apprehension of human (and divine) relations.

3. See Peter Brown, *Augustine of Hippo: A Biography* (Berkeley, CA: University of California Press, 1969.)

4. Augustine's biography is one of intense personal struggle to understand himself in relation to God. Reading his works and those of others about him, I'm left with the impression that his association of sex with sin was the result of his inability to control his sexual passion except through renunciation (see Miles, *Augustine on the Body* and *Fullness of Life*). I disagree with Miles that his response to his addiction—renunciation of the sins of the flesh—was not, thereby, repression. To the contrary, the case could be made that Augustine's repression of his sexuality constituted also his denial of the love of God as the erotic power that he experienced in relation to women (and to men); and that consequently, his legacy is indeed one of antagonism—not only to eros but also to God's love as our embodied, sensual desire to connect with one another. For a poignant, troubling glimpse into the life of a christian struggling against the erotic/power of God, see Augustine's *Confessions* (New York: Penguin, 1977), written in 397–398 C.E., at age forty-three.

5. As I write this chapter, I'm grateful especially to Tom F. Driver, my theological teacher, mentor, and friend, for encouraging me to push at the boundaries of acceptable theological discourse in trying to speak the truth of our lives-in-relation.

6. I wish to acknowledge the contributions of many of my students to this theological project. Especially, in this chapter, I would like to thank Anne Gilson, Rob Gorsline, Ellen Davis, Pat Shechter, Jeannette DeFriest, Lawrie Hurtt, Ann Wetherilt, Beth Marie Murphy, Diane Moore, Jenny Walters, Myke Johnson, and Linda Brebner.

7. The christian tendency to view history and "last things" or eschatology as linear is apt to block our view of the many dimensions of human and divine life. Christian theologians on the whole, in my opinion, understand the spiraling shape of eschatology less well than many feminist and womanist theorists writing from either nonchristian spiritual traditions or not explicitly as christians. See, for example, Starhawk, *The Spiral Dance: A Rebirth of the Ancient Religion of the Great Goddess* (San Francisco: Harper & Row, 1981), and *Truth or Dare: Encounters with Power, Authority and Mystery* (San Francisco: Harper & Row, 1987); Marge Piercy, *The Moon is Always Female* (New York: Alfred A. Knopf, 1985); Pam McAllister, ed., *Reweaving the Web of Life: Feminism and Non-Violence* (Philadelphia: New Society Publishers, 1982); Audre Lorde, *Sister Outsider: Essays and Speeches* (Trumansburg, NY: Crossing Press, 1984); and Carol Christ, *Laughter of Aphrodite: Reflections on a Journey to the Goddess* (San Francisco: Harper & Row, 1987).

8. *Christa*, a four-foot bronze female Christ on the cross, was sculpted by Edwina Sandys. It was displayed at the Episcopal Cathedral of St. John the Divine in New York City on April 19, 1984. "Eleven days later, after a storm of international protest, it was removed." Marian Christy, "Churchill's Controversial Granddaughter," *The Boston Sunday Globe* (January 22, 1989): A12.

9. Many resources, christian and other, are available for reimaging Christ as female. None is more remarkable, in my opinion, than Robin Morgan's "The Network of the Imaginary Mother," in *Lady of the Beasts* (New York: Random House, 1976). Christian theologians who are developing images of redemptive power as mediated through women include, among many others, Delores S. Williams, Rita Nakashima Brock, Sally McFague, and women such as the authors of *Inheriting Our Mothers' Gardens: Feminist Theology in Third World Perspective*, edited by Katie Geneva Cannon, Ada Maria Isasi-Diaz, Kwok Pui-Lan, and Letty M. Russell (Philadelphia: Westminster, 1988). Historians working toward the same theological purpose include Clarissa Atkinson, Marilyn Massey, Margaret R. Miles, Anne L. Barstow, E. Ann Matter, Fredrica Harris Thompsett, Eleanor McLaughlin, Barbara Brown Zikmund, and Joanne C. Brown. (This list is meant to be suggestive, not exhaustive.)

10. Coming to know, or understand, God—the business of theological education in its broadest sense—is a *relational* adventure in making, and understanding, right relation. See Paulo Freire, *Pedagogy of the Oppressed* (New York: Herder and Herder, 1970); Ira Shor and Paulo Freire, *A Pedagogy for Liberation: Dialogues on Transforming Education* (South Hadley, MA: Bergin and Garvey, 1987); Ira Shor, *Critical Teaching and Everyday Life* (Boston: South End Press, 1980); Alice Frazer Evans, Robert A. Evans, and William Bean Kennedy, *Pedagogies for the Non-Poor* (Maryknoll, NY: Orbis, 1987); Thomas P. Fenton, ed., *Education for Justice* (Maryknoll, NY: Orbis, 1975); Amanecida Collective, *Revolutionary Forgiveness: Feminist Reflections on Nicaragua* (Maryknoll, NY: Orbis, 1986); and MudFlower Collective, *God's Fierce Whimsy: Christian Feminism and Theological Education* (New York: Pilgrim, 1985).

11. When christian women have laid claim historically to sacred power, the ecclesiastical response has been punitive. Probably the most dramatic and large-scale violent response was the European witch hunt in the fifteenth and six-

teenth centuries. For bone-chilling testimony to the missionary zeal with which church fathers undertook this persecution, see *Malleus Maleficarum (Hammer of Witches)*, translated with introduction by the Rev. Montague Summers (New York: Dover, 1971). *Malleus* was published in 1456. Writing his introduction in 1928, Fr. Summers began with these words: "It has been recognized even from the very earliest times, during the first gropings towards the essential conveniences of social decency and social order, that witchcraft is an evil thing, an enemy to light, an ally of the powers of darkness, disruption, and decay." (xi)

12. See Isabel Carter Heyward, "Chalcedon's Ontology," Appendix B, in *The Redemption of God: A Theology of Mutual Relation* (Washington, D.C.: University Press of America, 1982), 189–92. My thanks to Richard A. Norris, with whom I worked occasionally at Union Theological Seminary, for helping me to wrestle with philosophical nuances in the christological controversy.

13. Elie Wiesel, *Night* (New York: Avon, 1969); Adrienne Rich, *On Lies, Secrets and Silence: Selected Prose, 1966–78* (New York: W. W. Norton, 1979); Julia Esquivel, *Threatened with Resurrection: Prayers and Poems of an Exiled Guatemalan* (Elgin, IL: Brethren, 1982); Gloria Naylor, *The Women of Brewster Place* (New York: Penguin, 1982); Lorde, *Sister Outsider*; Dorothee Sölle, *Beyond Mere Obedience, Reflections on a Christian Ethic for the Future* (Minneapolis: Augsburg, 1971); Beverly Wildung Harrison, *Making the Connections: Essays in Feminist Social Ethics*, edited by Carol S. Robb (Boston: Beacon, 1985).

14. See Richard Sennett and Jonathan Cobb, *The Hidden Injuries of Class* (New York: Random, 1973); Angela Y. Davis, *Women, Race, and Class* (New York: Vintage, 1981); Lillian B. Rubin, *Worlds of Pain: Life in the Working Class Family* (New York: Basic Books, 1976); Karen Stollard, *et al.*, *Poverty in the American Dream* (Boston: South End Press, 1983); Michelle Russell, "Women, Work, and Politics in the U.S.," *Theology in the Americas*, edited by Sergio Torres (Maryknoll, NY: Orbis, 1976); Barbara H. Andolsen, "A Woman's Work Is Never Done: Unpaid Household Labor as a Social Justice Issue," in Barbara Hilkert Andolsen, Christine E. Gudorf, and Mary D. Pellauer, eds., *Women's Consciousness, Women's Conscience* (San Francisco: Harper & Row, 1985), 3–18; and Nancy Bancroft, "Women in the Cutback Economy: Ethics, Ideology, and Class," in Andolsen, *et al.*, 19–31.

15. One of the best treatments of love in christian tradition, from a rather traditional perspective (though it does not solve the problems of the subordination of sexuality and friendship to "spiritual" love) is Daniel Day Williams, *The Spirit and the Forms of Love* (New York: Harper & Row, 1968). Williams presents a fluid rather than fixed distinction between the forms of love, in which sexual love (eros) has its fulfillment when directed beyond the realm of the particular bond between two people. Citing a work of Alfred Neumann, *Six of Them* (New York: Macmillan, 1945), Williams writes:

> Neumann . . . tells of a German professor of law who continued teaching in the early days of the Hitler regime, lecturing on justice with pointed reference to its subversion in the Nazi state. When fired from his position, the professor, his wife, and a loyal band of students publish secretly copies of his lec-

tures. . . . Six of them are caught, and tried in a Nazi kangaroo court. . . .
They are condemned to be executed. In the van in which they are being
taken to their death, the professor and his wife sit facing one another. They
have had a lifetime of love and work together. They are old now, their energies
exhausted by the struggle. Yet, as they look at one another, their love reaches
its highest moment. It has been consummated in the service of a cause which
transcends but does not negate personal *eros*. Sexual love has its fulfillment
in personal existence when it is thus transmuted. Sexuality must be shattered
in its self-centeredness and redirected to something greater. That it can be so
is a proof that this human love belongs with the creative action of *agape*.
(240)

For Williams, eros is a "self-centered" love that can be "redirected to something greater" and thus "belongs with the creative action of *agape*." This understanding differs from the concept of eros that, with Audre Lorde, I propose
in this book—namely, love that is by definition mutual, shared, and expansive
in its reach. Erotic love, as I understand it, *is* agapic. It can be distorted by
abusive power relations.

The most helpful treatments of love by christian feminists include Harrison,
"The Power of Anger in the Work of Love," in *Making the Connections*, 3–
21; Rita Nakashima Brock, *Journeys by Heart: A Christology of Erotic Power*
(New York: Crossroad Press, 1988); Dorothee Sölle with Shirley A. Cloyes, *To
Work and to Love: A Theology of Creation* (Philadelphia: Fortress, 1984); and
Embodied Love: Sensuality and Relationship as Feminist Values, edited by
Paula Cooey, Sharon Farmer, and Mary Ellen Ross (San Francisco: Harper &
Row, 1987).

The traditional christian understanding of love is summarized helpfully by
Gene Outka, *Agape: An Ethical Analysis* (New Haven: Yale University, 1972);
and is set forth by Anders Nygren, *Agape and Eros*, translated by Philip S.
Watson (London: S.P.C.K., 1957).

16. For more on transcendence, see Carter Heyward, "Crossing Over: On Transcendence," in *Our Passion for Justice* (New York: Pilgrim Press, 1984), 243–
47; Tom F. Driver, *Patterns of Grace: Human Experience or Word of God* (New
York: Harper & Row, 1977), in which Driver presents transcendence as "radical
immanence," 164, 165; Linell E. Cady, "Relational Love: A Feminist Christian
Vision," in Cooey, *et al.*, *Embodied Love*.

I am especially grateful to my friend and former student Ann Wetherilt for
several splendid conversations about transcendence during the 1988–89 academic year.

17. For attention to incarnation as embodied love, see James B. Nelson, *Embodiment: An Approach to Sexuality and Christian Theology* (Minneapolis: Augsburg, 1978); Heyward, *The Redemption of God*; Tom F. Driver, *Christ in a
Changing World: Toward an Ethical Christology* (New York: Crossroad, 1981);
Brock, *Journeys by Heart*; Harrison, "The Power of Anger in the Work of Love,"
and other essays in *Making the Connections*; and various pieces in Cooey, *et
al.*, *Embodied Love*, and Andolsen, *et al.*, *Women's Consciousness, Women's
Conscience*.

18. Dorothee Sölle, *Revolutionary Patience*, translated by Rita and Robert Kimber (Maryknoll, NY: Orbis, 1977).
19. Through her writing, our friendship, and our work together, Janet Surrey has helped me realize that we literally take shape with one another. See her essays in *Work in Progress* from the Stone Center for Developmental Services and Studies (Wellesley: Stone Center Working Paper Series): "Relationship and Empowerment" (1987); "Self-in-Relation: A Theory of Women's Development" (1985); "Eating Patterns as a Reflection of Women's Development" (1984); and with Judith V. Jordan and Alexandra G. Kaplan, "Women and Empathy—Implications for Psychological Development and Psychotherapy" (1983).
20. Lorde, "Uses of the Erotic: The Erotic as Power," *Sister Outsider*, 55, 56, 58.
21. *Ibid.*, 56.
22. *Ibid.*, 57–58.
23. *Ibid.*, 57.
24. *Ibid.*
25. Tom F. Driver, student of Paul Tillich and of Gestalt psychology, speaks of God as "ground and figure" in *Patterns of Grace*.
26. On theological language and imagery, see especially Nelle Morton, *The Journey Is Home* (Boston: Beacon, 1985); Mary Daly, *Beyond God the Father: Towards a Philosophy of Women's Liberation* (Boston: Beacon, 1973), and *Gyn/Ecology: The Metaethics of Radical Feminism* (Boston: Beacon, 1978); Harrison, "Sexism and the Language of Christian Ethics," in *Making the Connections*, 22–41; Linda Clark, Marian Ronan, and Eleanor Walker, *Image-Breaking, Image-Building: A Handbook for Creative Worship for Women of the Christian Tradition* (New York: Pilgrim, 1981); and Brian Wren, *What Language Shall I Borrow? God-Talk in Worship: A Male Response to Feminist Theology* (New York: Crossroad, 1989).
27. This reflects an existential apprehension of divine purpose. See Paul Tillich, *Systematic Theology*, three volumes in one (Chicago: University of Chicago, 1951), I, esp. Part II, II, B, "The Actuality of God," 235–89, in which Tillich discusses the creativity of the divine life.
28. I cannot overemphasize the extent to which "mutuality" can be understood adequately only insofar as we experience and conceptualize it as a way of describing *relational movement*. As such, it is not "a place to stay," not a static way of being.
29. See Margaret C. Huff, "The Interdependent Self: An Integrated Concept from Feminist Theology and Feminist Psychology," *Philosophy and Theology II*, no. 2: 160–72, on mutuality and other concepts from self-in-relation approach to psychology. Huff, Janet Surrey, Judith Jordan, Beverly Harrison, Ann Wetherilt, Sharon Welch, Demaris Wehr, and I have met regularly since early winter 1987, to explore the nuances of mutuality and other psychological and theological issues in our lives and work.
30. It is difficult not to idealize anything we value, especially when, as is often true with lesbian relationships, something has served as a vehicle for our healing or liberation. Still, I think that many lesbians, myself included, need to be

challenged always to speak honestly of our lives. To do so lends credibility and strength to our vision. A careful critique of power dynamics among ourselves *as women*, together with the refusal to gloss over our differences in the name of an idealized "unity," will tend to render an honest portrait of our lives-in-relation.

31. Feminist ethicist Norene M. Carter pointed out the eschatological character of erotic (mutual) power in my "Theology of Sexuality" class at the Episcopal Divinity School in spring 1988.

32. See chapter 3 on heterosexism for clarification of "alienated power," "alienation," and "structure."

33. Technically, *sadism* (after Count Donatien de Sade, France, 1740–1814) refers to "the getting of sexual (or other) pleasure from dominating, mistreating, or hurting one's partner (or others)." *Masochism* (after Leopold von Sacher-Masoch, Austria, 1835–1895) refers to "the getting of sexual (or other) pleasure from being dominated, mistreated, or hurt by one's partner (or others)." *Webster's New Twentieth-Century Dictionary*, unabridged (New York: William Collins and World: 1977 and 1975).

In this book, as in life, I am equating the exercise of power-over with domination and the experiencing of having power-under with that of being dominated. I am assuming, moreover, that sexually and otherwise, most people learn to associate enjoyment (physical or emotional pleasure) with one or both of these experiences since (1) relational dynamics of domination and submission shape the context of all our lives and (2) most, if not all, of us do find pleasure—sexual and/or other—in life.

34. Resources on sexual s/m in women's lives, especially in lesbian relationships, include Samois, ed., *Coming to Power: Writings and Graphics on Lesbian S/M* (Boston: Alyson, 1982), in which the authors define s/m as "a form of eroticism based on a consensual exchange of power" (title page); Robin Ruth Linden, Darlene R. Pagano, Diane E. H. Russell, and Susan Leigh Starr, eds., *Against Sadomasochism: A Radical Feminist Analysis* (East Palo Alto, CA: Frog in the Well, 1982). Robin Morgan's essay "Politics of Sado-Masochistic Fantasies," in *Going Too Far: The Personal Chronicle of a Feminist* (New York: Vintage, 1978), examines social roots of women's masochistic fantasies. Various of the authors in Carol S. Vance, ed., *Pleasure and Danger: Exploring Female Sexuality* (Boston: Routledge and Kegan Paul, 1984), examine the expanses and limits of female sexuality in the context of "pleasure and danger."

35. I am especially grateful to Ellen Davis and Bonnie Engelhardt for pushing against an oversimplification of lesbian s/m.

36. We feminists, especially those of us in healing professions, share a troubling and challenging quandary: How both to embody a nonabusive relational presence in which we respect our own and others' needs for privacy, space, and basic conditions for bodily integrity and, at the same time, to realize more and more fully that each of our "persons," our individual bodyselves, is being shaped in our relationships through mutually empowering processes of speaking, listening, touching, healing *with* one another? To use "boundaries" as walls behind which we withhold our real presence from those who seek our

help can be just as violent and abusive, emotionally and spiritually, as sexual abuse.

In attempting not to be abusive in our work, we ought not run from the goodness intrinsic to creative healing relationships in which both, or all, persons are moving toward the possibilities of embodying more fully mutual dynamics as we generate them together. We need to help one another learn how to do this—we priests, pastors, laypersons, therapists, clients, teachers, and students. Only together in community can we shape creative rather than damaging "boundaries."

37. Several pastoral resources on sexual abuse are Marie Marshall Fortune, *Sexual Violence: The Unmentionable Sin* (New York: Pilgrim, 1983); Ellen Bass, *I Never Told Anyone* (San Francisco: Harper & Row, 1983); Rita Lou Clark, *Pastoral Care of Battered Women* (Philadelphia: Westminster, 1986); Judith Herman, *Father-Daughter Incest* (Cambridge: Harvard University Press, 1981); and Mary D. Pellauer, *et al.*, *Sexual Assault and Abuse: A Handbook for Clergy and Religious Professionals* (San Francisco: Harper & Row, 1987).

38. See chapters 3 and 5 in Heyward, *The Redemption of God.*

39. "Mutual consent" really is a misnomer. It should be "equal consent" because it denotes an equality of power between or among individuals in reaching agreement. A child cannot "consent" in this way to having sex with an adult or with an older or stronger child. Similarly, adults cannot "consent" in a mutual way to having sex with those by whom they are, or feel, intimidated or threatened. For the purpose of discerning moral right and wrong in relation to having sex with younger people, a "child" is a young person (legally, someone under sixteen, eighteen, or twenty-one, depending upon the state) who does not have equal power in the relationship by which to say yes or no without feeling intimidated. For example, it might not be morally wrong for a seventeen-year-old to have sex with a fifteen-year-old, while it probably would be wrong for either of them to have sex with an eight- or ten-year-old.

While the law sets certain limits by defining age of mutual consent, it cannot determine moral right or wrong. Morality is about sharing power. It is not simply a matter of obeying the law. But we need to be clear that laws that protect children from sexual abuse are laws that emphatically serve the common good. These laws should be taken seriously in setting all guideposts for sexual behavior.

40. See note 36.

41. See Surrey, "Self-in-Relation: A Theory of Women's Development."

42. Personal conversation, December 1988.

43. Personal conversation, February 1989.

44. My friend Bridget Rees, English feminist and social justice activist, pointed this out in conversation, October 1987.

45. Our self-containment might be an experience of divine immanence provided we do not disconnect from one another.

46. Daly defines necrophilia as "attraction/need of males for female energy. . . , not in the sense of love for actual corpses, but of love for those victimized into a state of living death." Daly, *Gyn/Ecology*, 59.

47. Brock, *Journeys By Heart*, 69.

7. Undying Erotic Friendship: Foundations for Sexual Ethics

1. I am especially grateful in this chapter to Beverly Wildung Harrison for helping me envision and conceptualize these ethical foundations. The ethicists and moral philosophers upon whose work mine is most dependent are Beverly Wildung Harrison, *Making the Connections: Essays in Feminist Social Ethics*, edited by Carol S. Robb (Boston: Beacon, 1985); Daniel C. Maguire, *The Moral Choice* (Garden City, NY: Doubleday, 1978); H. Richard Niebuhr, *The Responsible Self* (New York: Harper & Row, 1963); John Macmurray, *The Forms of the Personal*, 2 vols., *Self as Agent, Persons in Relation* (London: Faber, 1957, 1961); and, from another realm and generation altogether, Frederick Denison Maurice (1805–1872) whose attention to Christian socialism, the value of women, the unity and inclusivity of the Kingdom [sic] of Christ, the conscience, and "the sense of righteousness in men [sic]" has informed my work.

   Other feminist/womanist ethicists whose work is important to me include Katie Geneva Cannon, *Black Womanist Ethics* (Atlanta: Scholars Press, 1988); Marvin M. Ellison, *The Center Cannot Hold* (Washington, D.C.: University Press of America, 1984); and Margaret A. Farley, *Personal Commitments: Beginning, Keeping, Changing* (San Francisco: Harper & Row, 1986).

2. Sexual abuse is evil. Having AIDS is not. It is important that the moral evil of sexual abuse perpetrated against women, children, and vulnerable men not be confused with the tragic disease of the HIV virus. In addition to the systemic evils in which the contagion is secured (racism, heterosexism, classism), the moral evil in the AIDS crisis is in the contemptuous, uncaring responses toward people with AIDS and, *to a far lesser degree*, the indifference on the part of some people with AIDS about whether their sexual partners contract the virus from them. (The latter concern needs to be considered in the context of all who have little or no concern for their sexual partners' health and well-being, such as men who are indifferent to women becoming pregnant.)

3. See chapter 3, page 58, and Chapter 4, page 65, for discussions of alienated sexuality.

4. Useful resources on AIDS include *The Surgeon General's Report on Acquired Immune Deficiency Syndrome* (Washington, D.C.: U. S. Department of Health and Human Services, 1988); "AIDS: A Special Issue," *Christianity and Crisis* 48, no. 10 (July 4, 1988); Cindy Patton, *Sex and Germs: The Politics of AIDS* (Boston: South End Press, 1985); Evelynn Hammonds, "Race, Sex, AIDS: The Construction of 'Other' " (28–36) and "Resistance and the Erotic: Reclaiming History, Setting Strategy as We Face AIDS" (68–78), *Radical America* 20, no. 6 (1987); Priscilla Alexander, "Prostitutes Are Being Scapegoated for Heterosexual AIDS," in *Sex Work: Writings by Women in the Sex Industry*, edited by Frederique Delacoste and Priscilla Alexander (San Francisco: Cleis, 1987); John E. Fortunato, *AIDS: The Spiritual Dilemma* (San Francisco: Harper & Row, 1987); Earl E. Shelp, Ronald H. Sutherland, Peter W. A. Mansell, M.D., *AIDS: Personal Stories in Pastoral Perspective* (New York: Pilgrim, 1986); John Snow, *Mortal Fear: Meditations on Death and AIDS* (Cambridge: Cowley, 1987).

5. See Farley, *Personal Commitments*, especially chapters 6 and 7, 67–109, on the relation of "obligation" to "commitment" and to "a just love."

6. For more on valuing our differences, see MudFlower Collective, *God's Fierce Whimsy: Christian Feminism and Theological Education* (New York: Pilgrim, 1985); Adrienne Rich, "Notes Toward a Politics of Location," *Blood, Bread and Poetry: Selected Prose, 1979–1985* (New York: W. W. Norton, 1986), 210–31; Audre Lorde, "The Master's Tools Will Never Dismantle the Master's House," in *Sister Outsider: Essays and Speeches* (Trumansburg, NY: Crossing Press, 1984); Elly Bulkin, Minnie Bruce Pratt, and Barbara Smith, *Yours in Struggle: Three Feminist Perspectives on Anti-Semitism and Racism* (Brooklyn, NY: Long Haul, 1984); Ada Maria Isasi-Diaz, "Toward an Understanding of *Feminismo Hispaño* in the U.S.A.," 51–61, and Judith Plaskow, "Anti-Semitism: The Unacknowledged Racism," 75–84, in Barbara Hilkert Andolsen, Christine E. Gudorf, and Mary D. Pellauer, eds., *Women's Consciousness, Women's Conscience: A Reader in Feminist Ethics* (San Francisco: Harper & Row, 1985).

7. Lee Hancock, "Incarnate Suffering and Faith," in "AIDS: A Special Issue," *Christianity and Crisis* 48, no. 10 (July 4, 1988).

8. There is enormous healing power in vulnerability. See Carter Heyward, *Our Passion for Justice: Images of Power, Sexuality and Liberation* (New York: Pilgrim, 1984), especially chapter 15, 123–31; chapter 27, 134–42; and chapter 29, 248–53. Also Harrison, *Making the Connections*, especially "The Power of Anger in the Work of Love," 3–21. Other resources include Rita Nakashima Brock, *Journeys By Heart: A Christology of Erotic Power* (New York: Crossroad, 1988); Dorothee Sölle, *Suffering* (Philadelphia: Fortress, 1973); and Starhawk, *Truth or Dare: Encounters with Power, Authority and Mystery* (San Francisco: Harper & Row, 1987).

9. Thomas Aquinas wrote,

> Virtue denotes some perfection of a power. The perfection of everything is estimated chiefly in regard to its end: now the end of power is action: hence a power is said to be perfect inasmuch as it is determined to its act. Now there are powers which are determined of themselves to their acts, as the active powers of physical nature. But the rational powers, which are proper to man, are not determined to one line of action, but are open indeterminately to many, and are determined to acts by habits. And therefore human virtues are habits.

> *Summa Theologica*, II–I, Q. 55, art. 1 (London: Burns Oats, 1986). The Thomist concept of virtue is of an individual man's (male's) "habit" or "possession" by which he is made good.

10. See chapter 3, page 48.

11. No ethic or theological conviction is generated out of nowhere. All of our values are socially constructed. In addition to the majority of feminist and liberation works cited in these notes, a book that explicates this motif is Georges Casalis, *Correct Ideas Don't Fall From the Skies: Elements for an Inductive Theology* (Maryknoll, NY: Orbis, 1984).

12. Several years ago, as we were discussing why the church has such a hard time affirming sex, Alison Cheek remarked matter-of-factly: "The church has never taught us that our bodies are good."

13. Beverly Harrison suggested these violations of bodily integrity in a program on sexuality and pastoral care at the Parkside Medical Center near Chicago in April 1988.

14. To be mutual in this way is to help create the conditions in which mutuality can thrive. As a way of describing love, mutuality is both here and coming; both now and not yet. See Christine E. Gudorf, "Parenting, Mutual Love, and Sacrifice," in Andolsen, et al., *Women's Consciousness, Women's Conscience,* 175–91, for splendid testimony to "mutual love."

15. See Farley, *Personal Commitments,* for careful work on faith and commitment. See also Heyward, "Sexual Fidelity," in *Our Passion for Justice,* 184–99.

16. Morton writes, "If one can be heard to one's own speech, then the speech would be a new speech and the new speech would be a new experience in the life of the speaker—that is, the one heard to speech." Nelle Morton, *The Journey Is Home* (Boston: Beacon, 1985), 202.

17. Lorde, "Uses of the Erotic: The Erotic as Power," *Sister Outsider,* 58–59.

18. Adrienne Rich, "Women and Honor: Some Notes on Lying," in *On Lies, Secret, and Silence: Selected Prose, 1966–1978* (New York: W. W. Norton, 1979), 192.

19. For two helpful presentations of the effective purposes of monogamy in the lives, primarily, of western white women, see Adrienne Rich, *Of Woman Born: Motherhood as Experience and Institution* (New York, W. W. Norton, 1976), especially chapter 5, 110–27; and Beverly Wildung Harrison, *Our Right to Choose: Toward a New Ethic of Abortion* (Boston: Beacon, 1983), especially chapter 3, 57–90.

20. Margaret Nichols, "Lesbian Sexuality: Issues and Developing Theory," in *Lesbian Psychologies,* edited by Boston Lesbian Psychologies Collective (Urbana and Chicago: University of Chicago Press, 1987), 97–125.

21. On friendship, there is a surplus of riches among feminists and womanists. For example, see Mary E. Hunt, *A Fierce Tenderness: Toward a Feminist Theology of Friendship* (San Francisco: Harper & Row, forthcoming 1990); Janice Raymond, *A Passion for Friends: Toward a Philosophy of Female Affection* (Boston: Beacon, 1986); Bulkin, et al., *Yours in Struggle*; Alice Walker, *The Color Purple* (New York: Harcourt Brace Jovanovich, 1982); Gloria Naylor, *The Women of Brewster Place* (New York: Penguin, 1983), and *Linden Hills* (New York: Ticknor and Fields, 1985); Ada Maria Isasi-Diaz and Yolanda Tarango, *Mujer Hispanica: Voz Profetica en la Iglesia: Hacia una Teologia de Liberacion (Hispanic Women: Prophetic Voice in the Church: Toward a Hispanic Women's Theology of Liberation)* (San Francisco: Harper & Row, 1988).

22. My good friend, spiritual mentor, and bishop, Robert L. DeWitt, has counseled many of us over the years "to keep our courage."

23. In September 1988, on our way home from an Outward Bound adventure on Maine's Penobscot Bay, Susan DeMattos said that she had learned from the experience that "our fear lies to us."

24. Heyward, *Our Passion for Justice,* 236–37.

25. See Amanecida Collective, *Revolutionary Forgiveness: Feminist Reflections on Nicaragua* (Maryknoll, NY: Orbis, 1986), for discussion of "forgiveness" from a relational perspective, especially chapter 4, 80–110.

26. See chapters 3 and 6, especially.
27. Beverly Wildung Harrison and I have been developing this framework of commitments in the course of our work together.
28. See Harrison, "The Power of Anger in the Work of Love," in *Making the Connections*, 3–21.

Glossary

1. A partial list of feminist liberation theologians and their works includes Barbara Hilkert Andolsen, Christine E. Gudorf, Mary D. Pellauer, eds., *Women's Consciousness, Women's Conscience: A Reader in Feminist Ethics* (San Francisco: Harper & Row, 1985); Rita Nakashima Brock, *Journeys By Heart: A Christology of Erotic Power* (New York: Crossroad, 1988); Elisabeth Schüssler-Fiorenza, *Bread Not Stone: The Challenge of Feminist Biblical Interpretation* (Boston: Beacon, 1984), and *In Memory of Her: A Feminist Theological Reconstruction of Christian Origins* (New York: Crossroad-Seabury Press, 1983); Beverly Wildung Harrison, *Making the Connections: Essays in Feminist Social Ethics*, edited by Carol S. Robb (Boston: Beacon, 1985); Ada Maria Isasi-Diaz and Yolanda Tarango, *Hispanic Women: Prophetic Voice in the Church* (San Francisco: Harper & Row, 1988); Mercy Amba Oduyoye, *Hearing and Knowing: Theological Reflections on Christianity in Africa* (New York: Orbis, 1986); Rosemary Radford Ruether, *Faith and Fratricide: The Theological Roots of Anti-Semitism* (New York: Seabury, 1974); *Sexism and God-Talk: Toward a Feminist Theology* (Boston: Beacon, 1983); *Womanguides: Readings Toward a Feminist Theology* (Boston: Beacon, 1985); Letty Russell, Kwok Pui-Lan, Ada Maria Isasi-Diaz, and Katie Geneva Cannon, eds., *Inheriting Our Mothers' Gardens: Feminist Theology in Third World Perspective* (Philadelphia: Westminster, 1988); and Letty Russell, ed., *Feminist Interpretation of the Bible* (Philadelphia: Westminster Press, 1985).

   The Episcopal Divinity School (EDS) in Cambridge, Massachusetts, is the only school in the United States that offers degrees in feminist liberation theology and ministry (FLTM). EDS offers Master of Arts and a Doctor of Ministry degrees in FLTM. In addition, Master of Divinity students can elect to direct their studies to this perspective and shape their programs accordingly.
2. See Mary E. Hunt, *A Fierce Tenderness: A Feminist Theology of Friendship* (San Francisco: Harper & Row, 1989), forthcoming, and Janice Raymond, *A Passion for Friends: Toward a Philosophy of Female Affection* (Boston: Beacon, 1986). See also chapter 7, note 21.
3. Isabel Carter Heyward, *The Redemption of God : A Theology of Mutual Relation* (Washington, D.C.: University Press of America, 1982).
4. Mary Daly pointed out that as divine be-ing God is a verb, not a noun. This was an important theme in my own book, *The Redemption of God*. Recently Virginia Ramey Mollenkott explored this in *Godding: Human Responsibility and the Bible* (New York: Crossroad, 1987).
5. *The Book of Common Prayer and Administration of the Sacraments and Other*

Rites and Ceremonies of the Church According to the Use of the Episcopal Church (New York: The Church Hymnal Corporation, 1979), 304.

6. This understanding of justice is one found throughout liberation theology: African American, Asian, Latin American, African, or jewish. See Allan Boesak, *Black and Reformed: Apartheid, Liberation and the Calvinist Tradition*, edited by Leonard Sweetman (New York: Orbis, 1984); Commission on Theological Concerns of the Christian Conference of Asia, ed., *Minjung Theology: People as Subjects of History* (New York: Orbis, 1981); James H. Cone, *A Black Theology of Liberation*, 2d ed. (New York: Orbis, 1986); Marc H. Ellis, *Toward a Jewish Theology of Liberation* (New York: Orbis, 1987); Deane William Ferm, ed., *Third World Liberation Theologies* (New York: Orbis, 1986); Gustavo Gutierrez, trans., Matthew J. O'Connell, *We Drink From Our Own Wells* (New York: Orbis, 1984), and *A Theology of Liberation: History, Politics and Salvation* translated and edited by Sister Coridad Inda and John Eagleson (Maryknoll, NY: Orbis, 1984). See also books in notes 1 and 11.

7. The concept and meaning of mutuality is an issue with which a number of theologians have wrestled. See Heyward, *The Redemption of God*; Reinhold Niebuhr, *The Nature and Destiny of Man: A Christian Interpretation* (New York: Scribner's Sons, 1953), particularly volume 2, chapter 3, 68–97; Daniel Day Williams, *The Spirit and the Forms of Love* (Digswell Place: James Nisbet and Co., Ltd., 1968).

Mutuality is an integral part of the work of the Stone Center, which understands mutuality as "a dynamic situation within relationship in which one is simultaneously open to the influence of the other or others, influencing the other or others, and aware of influencing the other or others. Both receptivity and active initiative are required, as are recognition and appreciation of the others' wholeness and particular experience." Margaret Craddock Huff, "The Interdependent Self: An Integrated Concept from Feminist Theology and Feminist Psychology," in *Philosophy and Theology II*, no. 2 (Winter 1987): 163.

Since writing *The Redemption of God* (1979–80), my understanding of mutuality has grown toward the realization that it is a relational movement rather than a place to be. To be mutual is to be changing and growing in relation to those who are changing and growing in relation to us. Moreover, mutuality involves a "calling forth" of one another to become more fully ourselves—in mutual relation.

8. Webster's *Third New International Dictionary* defines matrix as "something (as a surrounding or pervading substance or element) within which something else originates or takes form or develops." Philip Babcock Gove, Ph.D., ed., *Webster's Third New International Dictionary of the English Language*, unabridged (Springfield: G.C. Merriam Company, 1961).

9. "Power-over is linked to domination and control; power-from-within is linked to the mysteries that awaken our deepest abilities and potential. Power-with is social power, the influence we wield among equals.

Power-over comes from the consciousness I have termed estrangement: the view of the world as made up of atomized, non-living parts, mechanically interacting, valued not for what they inherently are but only in relation to some outside standard. It is the consciousness modeled on the God who stands outside the world, outside nature, who must be appeased, placated, feared, and above all, obeyed.

Starhawk, *Truth or Dare: Encounters with Power, Authority and Mystery* (San Francisco: Harper & Row, 1987), 9.
10. Martin Buber, *I and Thou*, translated by Walter Kaufman (New York: Charles Scribner's Sons, 1970), 69.
11. Alice Walker, *In Search of Our Mothers' Gardens* (San Diego: Harcourt, Brace, Jovanovich, 1983), xi. See also Katie G. Cannon, *Black Womanist Ethics* (Atlanta: Scholars Press, 1988).
12. Walker, *In Search of Our Mothers' Gardens*, xii.

GLOSSARY

In this book, I'm using some old words in new ways as well as some terms the reader may not know. This glossary by no means covers the entire range of terms in this book that may have varying meanings for different readers. It includes words that seem to me most likely to need working definitions.

erotic The erotic is our desire to taste and smell and see and hear and touch one another. It's our yearning to be involved—all "rolled up"—in each other's sounds and glances and bodies and feelings. The erotic is the flow of our senses, the movement of our sensuality, in which we experience our bodies' power and desire to connect with others. The erotic moves transpersonally among us and also draws us more fully into ourselves.

Although, to some extent, everyone's eroticism is distorted by abusive power relations (of domination and control), the erotic is the sacred/godly basis of our capacity to participate in mutually empowering relationships.

Abusive power relations teach us to be afraid of our erotic power—afraid, that is, of one another and of our own creative/liberating power in relation. In learning to fear the erotic, we resist relating intimately with one another. In addition, we are cut off from knowing and loving ourselves very well, because self-knowledge and self-love, very much like the knowledge and love of God, is available only in right, mutual relation with others.

feminist liberation theology Feminist liberation theology is a theological movement that has developed during the last two decades among women in Euroamerican cultures who understand feminism to be a shared commitment to the well-being of women of all classes, cultures, religions, colors, racial/ethnic heritages, ages, and sexual preferences; and to justice for poor men, men of color, gay-men, and other men who suffer oppression.[1] With the passage of time, and with education in the complexities of global economic and other social realities, increasing numbers of feminist theologians are becoming feminist liberation theologians.

Many feminist liberation theologians work conceptually to mend splits between nature and history, spirituality and politics, the collective good and personal well-being, theory and action, human justice and the good of all creation, and other points of tension not always addressed by feminist or liberation theologies.

Many feminist liberation theologians have benefited from studying Marxian social, political, and economic theory. Many are interested also in developing an adequate social analysis as foundational for pastoral counseling, psychotherapy, spiritual direction, and other traditionally one-to-one healing relationships.

friendship Among feminist philosophers and liberation theologians, the word friendship is used frequently as a synonym for right, mutual, relation.[2] This is because, for many women, friendship is the most exact experience we have of mutual relationship. For many of us, heterosexual as well as lesbian, our friendships with women, whether lovers or not, are more genuinely erotic than our marriages or relationships with male lovers.

In this book, I use the experience and concept of friendship as a paradigm for mutual relation, for justice in the small daily places of our lives as well as an image for justice and "godding" in the world. Nothing matters more.

God/the sacred God is our power in mutual relation.[3] It is with and by this sacred power that we are able to nurture relationships as resources of growth as cocreative women and men. By God, we can act, responsibly (morally/ethically) and joyfully, on behalf of the liberation of all people and creatures, including ourselves, from bondage to wrong relation.

God, our sacred power, is both "personal" and "transpersonal." God is the active source of our creative, liberating power—she with whom we are open (in prayer). We embody the Sacred when we generate right relation, acting with one another as resources of the divine Spirit. Insofar as we do so, we "god" (verb). We can image and know God/the Sacred as "person" *and* as an "impersonal" spirit that moves among us.

In christian tradition, God's "personal" presence has been most popularly imaged as that of a "Father" and his "Son," Jesus/Christ. God's "impersonal" way of being has been as a less image-bound spiritual presence among us. The ancient christian doctrine of the Trinity suggests that God the Holy Spirit is the spiritual connection between God the Father and God the Son. The value of this trinitarian schema is its implicit recognition of the dynamic relationality *in* God as well as between God, Jesus, and the rest of us. Although patristic christianity ignored the radically relational implications of its own insight, such a god can't be readily boxed into any single image or person, since God is both source and movement, incarnate in persons and a spiritual force that cannot be contained in any single human life, including that of Jesus.

The androcentric character of christianity makes it difficult or impossible for many self-respecting women to relate affirmatively to Jesus, the Trinity, or other patriarchal doctrines. We need not be christian to experience the dynamic, relational movement of the Sacred, whose images are as many and various as the women who know and love her.

In any given time or place, God can be experienced most "personally" among people who are living in or struggling for right relation—even if we are alone. We do not have to be physically present to one another to know ourselves connected. Much strength in solitude is derived from our memory of, awareness of, and hope for personal experience of embodied mutuality. From a feminist liberation perspective, God is experienced, known, and celebrated—through presence and solitude—as the power moving for justice and friendship among all human and other creatures in great and small places of our life together.

By this power, we god. Godding, we experience our personal lives as profoundly connected at the root of who we are, rather than as separate and disconnected from our professional lives and from one another's places of deepest meaning. Godding, we share how we really feel and what we really think about our bodyselves-in-relation, in our living and working, our living and dying. We share, we act, we are, together.[4]

This book is not intended to be necessarily, or even primarily, for christians. It is, however, a "christian book" because I am a christian working on the basis of several commitments, including a promise to "persevere in resisting evil and, whenever [I] fall into sin, [to] repent and return to God."[5]

I am mindful that I "fall into sin" whenever I participate in denying or violating right relation in the small and large places of my daily life, often when I am least aware of it and sometimes when I believe that I am doing what is right. The words on these pages come as sacred call to me, no less than to you, to resist evil and welcome goodness into our life together on the earth.

good and sin/evil God is the source and constant resource of good in our lives. Right, mutual, relation is good. Justice is good. Friendship is good. Sensuality, eroticism, and unalienated sexuality are good. Whatever is good creates *more* mutuality, *more* justice, *stronger* friendship.

Evil festers in our sin, which is our denial or violation of right relation, our rejection of movement toward mutuality. In feminist liberation theology, good and evil are at root systemic problems: racism is evil, antiracist struggle is good; heterosexism is evil, working for sexual and gender justice is good.

justice Justice is the shape of mutuality in our life together, in our societies and relationships—friendships, families, local and larger communities, the world itself. This concept is derived from jewish and christian traditions, in which the "righteousness" (Hebrew, *hesed*) of God—God's justice—is reflected in human justice to the extent that we are willing participants in creating God's justice on the earth among ourselves: God is in right relation with us, that is, if we are open to being in right relation with God. If we are, we can see in our relationships with one another reflections of God.[6] Justice is the actual shape of love in the world.

mutuality Mutuality is the process of loving and is a way of speaking of love.[7] It is the experience of being in right relation. *Mutuality is sharing power in such a way that each participant in the relationship is called forth more fully into becoming who she is—a whole person, with integrity.*

Experientially, mutuality is a process, a relational movement. It is not a static place to be, because it grows with/in the relationship. As we are formed by mutuality, so too does the shape of our mutuality change as our lives-in-relation grow. We become bearers with one another of the justice of God. Not perfectly, but authentically.

person/al A "person" emerges from within a relational matrix, or womb.[8] There is so such thing as simply an "individual" person, separate from others. Our lives are connected—spiritually, politically, economically, psychologically. To be a person is to be related. Thus our "personal" lives are not simply "private." Our personal lives bear profound political implications. Our personal lives are connected to one another's and to events and processes in the larger, public world in which we live. My *bodyself* is me. There is no split between my "self" and my "body" or between the core of my identity as a person-in-relation and my sensuality.

power Power is the ability to move, effect, make a difference; the energy to create or destroy, call forth or put down. Outside of a particular context, power bears neither positive nor negative connotations. Power can be used for good or for ill. Using *power-with* others is good. Using *power-over* others is evil.[9]

From a feminist/womanist liberation perspective, Oliver North's power was used for evil—his military status, his accessibility to the president, his role with the National Security Council, his efforts to finance and organize the contras, and so on. Whether power is good or bad depends upon whose interest it serves and for what purpose. *Power-with serves to further empower all persons in a relationship. Power-over serves to further empower a few and disempower others.* Power in the hands of a rapist, a batterer, or a murderer, or in the service of greed, duplicity, or cruelty is evil power. Power for liberation from despair, suffering, or injustice is good power. We have all used power for good and for evil, and we always will. Still, we can learn with one another's encouragement what it means to have power-with one another, to share and use our power for good.

Christian women, contrary to what the church has taught us to be possible, must learn to experience our power to connect with one another as good power, and also our power to connect with our own bodyselves. We have much relational power: our power to decide whether to give birth; our power to feel deeply and think clearly and well about people and places and ideas; our power to desire sexually; our power to befriend—to be in mutual relation with—men and women; our power to name our own lives, dreams, feelings, ideas, values, visions, talents, interests, passions, god/esses. Experienced as an energy to connect with one another on behalf of whatever may strengthen the fabric of our commonlife, our power is relational, it is erotic, and it is good. Our womanpower in relation is sacred power. It is God's power.

relation Relation is where it all begins, life and love and work and pleasure and pain—our selves. As Buber wrote, "In the beginning is the relation."[10] We come into this world connected, related, to one another—by blood and tissue, history, memory, culture, faith, joy, passion, violence, pain, and struggle. The lines of continuity between and among us are visible/invisible, sturdy/fragile, inviting/frightening, delightful/sad, occasions for celebration/remorse, depending on which connections we know best, or seek, or acknowledge, or explore.

To be related is essentially good, but not all relationships are good. There is right relation, that which is in fact true to itself—relation in which all parties are empowered to be more fully who they are as persons (or creatures) in relation. There is wrong relation, that which is literally perverse, "turned around" from its own possibility, distorted. In such a relation, all persons or participants are not empowered to be themselves. One or more are disempowered—trivialized, diminished, abused—in and by the relation. Wrong relation is the root of evil in our life together. Its causes are myriad, though fear of our humanness—fear of the scope and depth and passion of our relational possibilities—plays a primary role in precipitating and cementing wrong relation.

sensuality *Sensuality is our embodied feelings.* It is the mingling of our senses and emotions, the channel through which we feel, for example, either heat or pain. We are sensual persons: we touch and enjoy; taste and delight; hear and get angry; smell and are excited; see and fear.

Our daily lives are limitless resources of sensuality, occasions for strong, embodied feelings as parents, musicians, miners, painters, and health care practitioners; janitors, weavers, woodspersons, playwrights, and public servants; domestic workers, sculptors, students, soldiers, dancers, and draftspersons; garbage collectors, nannies, cooks, cabbies, poets, and plumbers.

We work with our bodies, in our bodies, as bodies, sensual bodyselves working, playing, making love, making justice, making sense with our hands, tongues, noses, eyes, toes, and ears. Whether or not we are aware of it (and much of our spiritual problem is that patriarchal religion has taught us to be unaware of this), our sensuality provides our relational grounding. It keeps us in touch with one another and with who we are.

Sensuality is a frightening reality for those who prefer to live "in their heads." Our passion, our capacities for pain and pleasure, and our will to change are rooted in our sensuality.

sexuality *Sexuality is our embodied, relational response to erotic/*

sacred power. We often locate our sexuality in our genitals, since we often "feel sexual" between our legs when we are erotically stimulated by a person, a memory, a song, a possibility . . .

Sex refers to our "touching toward" one another's genitals. We "have sex" when our embodied, relational response to our erotic power is to stimulate each other's bodyselves physically—including frequently, but not necessarily, and not only, our genital organs.

Sexuality, in our historical moment and location, refers most commonly to our experience of the *relational context* in which we desire to "have sex," to express sexually our embodied relational power: with others, with ourselves alone, with women, with men, with both women and men, with or without genital contact . . .

Like erotic power, our sexualities to some degree are distorted by the power relations of domination and control that pervade the world in which we live. In this context, sexuality can be "perverted" ("turned completely around" from its erotic purpose). It can become violent (as in cases of rape, incest, and other forms of sexual abuse) and/or can become associated primarily with pain or fear.

In summary, sensuality is the embodied basis of our feelings; it involves the mingling of our "senses" (taste, touch . . .) and our "emotions" (hurt, joy, anger . . .). The erotic is our sacred sensual *movement,* for example, from loneliness to yearning to fear to desire to touch. It is the relational source of our creativity/liberation. Sexuality is our embodied, relational response to erotic power, which often (but not always) involves sharing genital pleasure.

womanism This term originates in the work of Alice Walker. It is not simply "black feminism," but rather signifies black women's reality.[11] Womanist theologians such as Delores Williams and Katie Cannon, though as scholars and educators they frequently identify their work as feminist liberation theology, invite attention to their profoundly womanist perspectives. Other women of color, Asian and Latina as well as African American, often share with womanists a focus on the particularity of their racial/ethnic roots and values in the context of imperialistic anglo assumptions that manage to seep through even much of the best feminist liberation theology done by anglo (or other white) women. Walker suggests that "feminism is to womanism as lavender is to purple."[12] Womanism is about color and passion, liberation and celebration. It does not seek approval from the men (or women) of any color who hold unjust power in place.